Lost in Cyberspace?

Robert Chodos, Eric Hamovitch,
Rae Murphy

16 01 01

James Lorimer & Company, Publishers
Toronto, 1997

We acknowledge the support of the Canada Council for the Arts for our publishing program.

Photograph by Findlay Muir

Canadian Cataloguing in Publication Data

Chodos, Robert, 1947–

Lost in cyberspace?
Includes index.

ISBN 1-55028-519-x (bound)
ISBN 1-55028-518-1 (pbk.)
1. Information society - Canada.
  2. Computers and civilization.
  I. Murphy, Rae, 1935–
  II. Hamovitch, Eric. III. Title.

HM221.C46 1997 303.48'34'0971   C97-930933-6

James Lorimer & Company Ltd., Publishers
35 Britain Street
Toronto, Ontario
M5A 1R7

Printed and bound in Canada

Contents

Preface

This is the fourth book that the three of us have written in collaboration, and each subsequent book has in a sense emerged out of the one before. We began with *Selling Out* (1988), a critique of the first term of Brian Mulroney's government, where we concluded that the unifying theme in the government's policies, from free trade to Meech Lake to immigration, was a devotion to corporate interests, to the "bottom line." With the dramatic events of 1990 — the collapse of Meech Lake, the Oka confrontation, the election of the NDP in Ontario, the uproar over the Goods and Services Tax — the time seemed ripe to update and expand this analysis. In *The Unmaking of Canada* (1991), we argued that the pattern we had discerned in *Selling Out* was not unique to the Mulroney government but formed part of a tendency that ran through postwar Canadian history, in which the key element was continental integration. By 1990, the operation of this tendency had seriously weakened the underpinnings of Canada's existence as a country.

We also suggested that while specifically Canadian factors were certainly at work, there was also a global dimension to Canada's malaise. This was the theme that we pursued in our next book, *Canada and the Global Economy* (1993). We came to the conclusion that the global economy is not in itself a bad thing, and in any case is here to stay. But we did argue against the dominant form of globalization, which serves the interests of multinational corporations and is abetted by compliant governments under the rubric of the free market and laissez-faire. In early 1994, this line of thinking led us to begin taking serious note of the information highway, which like its cousin the global economy is not good or bad in itself but can be put to a variety of uses.

Many of the books that have been written about the information highway are instructional: what kind of equipment to get and how to use it. Necessary and valuable as much of this literature is, it is not our purpose here to add to it. Another genre of writing about the information highway seeks to predict the form it will take. Will people download books from online bookstores and print them out at home? Will everyone run their lives with wallet-sized personal computers that they carry around in their purses or pockets, as Bill Gates of Microsoft foresees? Will surgeons perform long-distance operations using virtual reality technology?

We don't profess to know. Nor do we believe these are the most important questions to ask. We agree with the information gurus quoted at the beginning of Chapter 1 that, despite all the hype, the scale of the change brought on by the information highway is probably being underestimated. But we are not persuaded by some of the ideas that often accompany the hype: that this change is wholly beyond human control, or that its implementation is best left to the benign workings of the "free market." There is an urgent public interest in the information highway, and an important role for public authorities in promoting and protecting that interest.

Because of the pace of change, the public interest may sometimes be difficult to tease out of the tangle of issues involved. Because electronic communications technology has little respect for borders, in some cases the public authorities that could act most effectively are international ones that do not yet exist. Nevertheless, we see the most significant questions raised by the information highway as being ones of public policy and social concern, and these questions are our focus in this book.

It is paradoxical but perhaps understandable that, faced with this rapid pace of change, we have been slower in bringing this book to completion than any of our previous ones. Each day's news brought word of a new Internet application, a projected corporate merger, or some other development that seemed important to take into account. Finally we decided that the moving target we were aiming at was never going to stand still and we couldn't keep updating the manuscript forever. By the time you read this book some of the specific information in it will no doubt be obsolete. But we have also found that the underlying issues — the effects of technology on employment, the need to bring some concept of the public interest into play, the importance of providing for broad public access — have not really changed in the more than three years we have been following the information highway. These issues are our real subject, and they are what we hope you will retain from accompanying us on our journey through cyberspace.

Robert Chodos
Rae Murphy
Eric Hamovitch

1

Highway, Railway or Goat Track?

I don't think this is the most profound change since the Industrial Revolution. I think it's the most profound technological shift since the capture of fire.

John Perry Barlow

Information superhighways are one of those rare technologies that are actually far more powerful and promising than the hype surrounding them.

George Gilder

Everything, absolutely everything, is up for grabs, and nothing is going to make any sense at all for a couple of decades. So you may as well sit back and enjoy the ride.

Paul Saffo

When Canada's Parliament opened early in 1994, soon after the election that brought Jean Chrétien's Liberals to power, the Speech from the Throne contained a reference that many Canadians found puzzling. The government, it said, would develop a strategy for the information highway.

"Information highway" was not exactly a household expression in 1994, although people were accustomed to hearing about at least some parts of what it signified. Advances in the field of computers had received considerable media play. Many people were also aware of a coming proliferation of television channels, whether by satellite or by cable. To a lesser extent, people were familiar with the idea of new services coming over their telephone wires. But consciousness of something called the information highway, which seemed to combine elements of all of these developments, was not widespread.

Over the next two years, that situation would change: the information highway became one of the favoured media topics of the mid-1990s. Coined in 1988 by Al Gore, now vice president of the United States, the term generally refers to a basket of new communications technologies, including 500-channel cable or satellite television, movies on demand, pocket-sized personal communications devices, videoconferencing, medical databases and virtual reality computers that allow for remote-control operations, online newspapers and magazines, and the anarchic global network of computer networks known as the Internet. To be sure, some of the details have remained a bit vague, and there has been no general agreement on what is part of the information highway and what isn't. Indeed, discussion of the information highway has largely focused on two separate but related topics.

One topic concerns the activities of corporations, especially telephone companies (telcos) and cable television companies (cablecos), that have been moving into new fields of endeavour: in Canada primarily Rogers Cablesystems, which took over Maclean Hunter in 1994, and the Stentor group of telephone companies, consisting of Bell Canada, B.C. Telephone and the rest. The activities of these corporate giants are seen to represent a convergence of the broadcasting and telecommunications industries. The "information highway" in this vision is largely a delivery system for providing ever-larger amounts of entertainment or "infotainment," some of it "interactive," in an increasing diversity of formats.

The other topic frequently discussed in relation to the highway is computer networks. The highway has been identified with the growth of computer networks and most particularly with the Internet, which has expanded rapidly from its military, government and academic origins to widespread general use, especially in North America but in other parts of the world as well. Initially developed without any significant corporate presence, the Internet has grown to encompass millions of users. It has become a major media phenomenon and has in some ways entered the popular culture.

Many predictions made about the new technologies have made the mistake of focusing on only part of the picture and as a result have soon been overtaken by events. In 1979, journalist Glenn Schneider wrote a rather prescient article in which he foresaw widespread electronic mail and online libraries — but not the personal computer.[1] A book called *The Information Superhighway: Beyond the Internet* by computer journalist Peter Otte, published in early 1994, failed to mention the World Wide Web, soon to become both the fastest-growing part of the Internet and the feature most responsible for bringing it into the mainstream. An Ottawa regulator interviewed by one of the authors in early 1995 did not consider the Internet worth her attention because it was "narrowband" — in other words, it did not transmit large enough quantities of data to compete seriously as an entertainment medium. Not only were all these assertions and omissions wrong, but they also reflected a mindset that sees the information highway as essentially a passive entertainment medium and therefore underestimates its real potential. This mindset was well described by economist George Gilder:

> A Hughes Aircraft Corp. rocket's red glare in French Guiana, bombs bursting in air on 500 channels, give proof through the night that something is going on out there: 150 choices of DirecTV broadcast satellite images; up to one billion hertz of cable TV bandwidth; star-spangled malls of infomercials; CD radio with fidelity beyond the ken of the human ear; high-reso-lution wrestlemania; 3,000 films on-demand; interactive per-sonals and impulse pay-per-view playmates; Yellow Pages blooming into home-shopping bonanzas; and videogames ga-lore on compact discs and cartridges. All zooming through the air, blasting through cable and pulsing through fiber at the speed of light. All to be captured, decrypted, decompressed, rendered and rolled out from the new set-top boxes, game players and supertheaters in millions of colors and living rooms.
>
> In such a phantasmagoria, what could be missing? The same thing that is missing in much of the media coverage of the information superhighway: the personal computer.[2]

Gilder emphasizes the importance of the hardware. The machine chosen as our link to the information highway is key: will it be the computer or the television set? For IBM or Microsoft or Sony, billions of dollars ride on this question. For the rest of us, the hardware question is a window onto more fundamental questions of what the information highway is for and who will control it.

The television set, no matter how "interactive" it is, even if it has a "set-top box" to allow users to personalize newscasts and download movies at their convenience, is an essentially passive device. An information highway based on television is primarily a medium for giving us more of the kind of service provided by television for the last four decades. We may be able to choose what movies we want to see and when we want to see them. We may be able to order up custom-designed newscasts emphasizing the particular stories we are interested in. But in the end, we remain consumers, and the flow of information over the highway remains overwhelmingly one-way.

For the visionaries of the Internet, this is far from being enough. Here is Michael Strangelove, author of *How to Advertise on the Internet*:

> The Internet is a new form of mass communication. Mass communication, while itself a relatively new phenomenon, has always involved controlled broadcasts to passive audiences. The mass audience has never had any significant input, or control, over the content of mass communication.
>
> With the Internet these characteristics of mass communication have forever changed. On the Net we find massive numbers of people broadcasting information to massive numbers of people. Whereas the introduction of the Gutenberg Press made mass communication possible for the very, very few who would ever own a printing press, the Internet has turned every owner of a computer, a modem, and a telephone line into a publisher, a radio station, and soon enough, a TV studio. This is the second Gutenberg revolution. This is the new economy of information.[3]

There are problems with this vision, as we will see. But we agree with Strangelove that the information highway has the potential to change people's lives for the better only to the extent that it grows as a two-way medium. What kind of information highway we will have has not yet been determined, and whether it will be one-way or two-way is one of the major issues remaining to be settled.

Technology and Corporate Organization

Many terms have been used, and sometimes overused, to designate the information flows that are being augmented by novel technologies such as the Internet and direct-to-home satellite television. *Information highway* and *information superhighway* are among the most commonly heard. These are occasionally shortened, especially in the United States, to the German-sounding *infobahn*, although the more French-sounding term *inforoute* has the merit in Canada of making sense in both official languages.

As the metaphor has penetrated the public consciousness, highway imagery has proliferated. There have been on ramps and off ramps, lanes, parking areas and hundred-car pileups. The imagery makes sense at least insofar as we accept the analogy between information flows and superhighways, with their multiple lanes and high speeds. As most Internet users know, however, this so-called superhighway may sometimes be likened more accurately to a narrow dirt road ("information goat track" is one term that has been suggested); speeds are often anything but fast.

Another problem with this analogy is that access to the most fundamental communications channels are controlled more tightly than the entry to most highways. Almost everybody in Canada has access to basic telephone service, and phone companies seldom try to control who uses the phone, but try setting up a rival service using the telephone company's network and see how far you get. Or see what kind of welcome you get from cable TV companies if you try to use their coaxial cables for any service other than what they choose to provide.

You'll feel pretty much as you would if you tried to marshal a train and run it down somebody else's track. Railway companies do not take kindly to competition on their tracks; they issue running rights to competitors only reluctantly. While highways are open to just about any vehicle that meets basic licensing requirements, railways most decidedly are not. In reality, the inforoute is more like a railway than a highway insofar as communications companies own the basic infrastructure and control who gets to use it. In this regard, what we are are encountering, even as we prepare to enter the twenty-first century, might be more accurately called an information railway. In the past half-century, highways have unambiguously eclipsed railways in freight and passenger traffic; access is one of the reasons for this. As we shall see in Chapter 3, the information railway we have now is not necessarily the model we should keep.

Furthermore, the highway metaphor implies that something as yet nonexistent will be built: a great electronic trunk line, to which our houses and offices will be connected and into which we can plug our telephones, computers, fax machines and TVs. There may be such a highway at some point, and there may not. It seems likely that a variety of communication channels — telephone wires, coaxial cables, electromagnetic waves transmitted through the air — will continue to exist for some time. The capacity of these channels will grow, and they will carry new kinds of information and entertainment. You may get movies over your telephone wire and send faxes over your TV cable. But the multiplicity of technologies will remain. In that sense the term *information infrastructure*, used in a landmark U.S. government document in 1993, is probably better than information highway, even if it doesn't lead to the same proliferation of images.

Whatever we call it, the force underlying current developments is the convergence of what have historically been separate technologies, and fundamental to convergence is digitalization. Until now, electronic transmission has been mostly an analogue process: continuous signals mimic the original data, sound or pictures. Electronic communication — from the telegraph and the telephone through radio and television broadcasting to the fax machine — converts the data, sound or pictures to such signals at the originating terminal, transmits the signals through a wire or wireless medium, and then converts them back to their original form at another terminal at some other location, across town or across the ocean. For administrative reasons as much as technical ones, each form of communication was assigned its own transmission medium — twisted-pair copper wire for telephones, electromagnetic waves for radio and later for television, then coaxial cable for television as well.

Computers, on the other hand, process information in the form of digits or "bits": 0s and 1s. Mathematical equations, text, pictures and sound can all be converted to 0s and 1s instead of analogue signals. Whatever the bits originally were, computers — or other terminals with the necessary computing capability — can deal with them once they are in the form of 0s and 1s. Digital media allow for much greater flexibility than analogue ones. Thus, digital compact discs (CDs) can be used to store music, computer programs or films. Digital reproduction also generally allows higher quality than analogue reproduction, the recent nostalgia-laden vogue for vinyl records notwithstanding.

Furthermore, bits can be electronically transmitted. Once a book, movie or symphony is digitalized, it can be sent from one terminal to another. Given enough transmission capacity or "bandwidth," this transmission can take place in seconds. Ideally, the transmission medium itself is digital. This is the case with fibre optic cable — extremely fine ribbons of glass over which bits travel in the form of pulses of light. However, analogue transmission media such as twisted-pair copper wire or coaxial cable can be used as well. The terminal will then need a device to convert bits to analogue signals so that they can be transmitted, and convert incoming analogue signals back to bits so that they can be processed. This is how a modem (*mo*dulator-*dem*odulator) makes it possible for a computer to function as a communications device using ordinary telephone wire.

With digitalization and with the telephone, broadcasting and cable companies aiming to become integrated "telecommunications" corporations, the logic behind restricting each form of communication to a particular transmission medium has been breaking down. Whether it's voice, data, text or pictures that you want to send, a variety of transmission possibilities are available, at least in theory. The advantage of fibre optic cable is that it offers much more bandwidth than either coaxial cable or especially telephone wire. On the other hand, copper telephone wire provides entry into a lot more homes and offices than fibre, which at the moment is used primarily for long-distance trunk lines and can be universally installed only at great expense.

Coaxial cable, which reaches most homes in North America and has several times the bandwidth of copper wire, would seem to offer the best of both worlds. However, the coaxial cable network currently in place was designed for one-way communication — television broadcasting — and would need to be re-engineered if it were to function as part of a two-way inforoute. It was only in 1995 that cable companies began to promote limited two-way service.

Wireless media — satellites broadcasting direct-to-home television, personal digital communications devices that can transmit and receive voice, pictures or data from the house, car, beach or golf course, perhaps hundreds of low-orbit satellites facilitating computer communications — are part of the overall schema as well. In the 1980s, Nicholas Negroponte of the Media Lab at the Massachusetts Institute of Technology predicted what became known as the "Negroponte Switch" — what went by air (television) would switch to wire; what went by wire (telephone) would switch to air. With the growth of cable TV and cellular phones, this has come to pass to a degree, but what seems to be emerging is a picture in which all forms of communication travel through both wire and wireless media.

How is all this to be organized? At one time, telephones, television and computers were essentially separate industries and each had its own cosy oligopoly. In the telephone and broadcasting industries, government regulation by the Canadian Radio-television and Tele-communications Commission (CRTC) in Canada and the Federal Communications Commission (FCC) in the United States helped keep the oligopolies in place and ensured that the services they provided bore some relationship to what these bodies perceived as being in the public interest.

In the 1980s, technological developments combined with the resurgence of classical liberal economics, under which "deregulation" and "competition" became buzzwords, began to blur the boundaries among the different industries and crack the oligopolies. Companies such as American Telephone and Telegraph (AT&T) in the United States and Bell Canada agreed to the introduction of competition in their traditional telephone business in exchange for being allowed to enter some of the newer and more glamorous telecommunications fields. In the 1990s, real and proposed mergers and joint ventures among telcos, cablecos, film studios, television networks, computer software makers and other related companies have been a staple of business news.

In the current ideological climate, virtually everyone favours competition, but competition can mean a number of different things. Most often, competition is presented in terms of choice. As communications writer Dana Blankenhorn sees it, competition provides consumers — in this case Emory University in Atlanta — with services they would not otherwise have:

> This is about competition. If this is going to really happen, I want a choice. I don't want to take Coke if I happen to prefer Pepsi. Emory has Coke and Pepsi. They needed fast data lines. Southern Bell said no way. The university went to their alternate carrier, MFS, and asked for a fiber loop, and MFS said they could do it. Right after they got approval for the bid, Southern Bell came back and said, "Oh, sure, we can do it." Competition.[4]

However, one of the implications of competition is that if the competitors are left to their own devices, one of them may drive the others out of business, so that in the end even Pepsi partisans have no choice but to drink Coke. Radical free marketers such as George Gilder are willing to accept this implication:

To the Washington regulators and their elected allies, competition has always meant rivalry between the existing competitors — long distance, broadcast, Baby Bells and Cable TV — and the regulation succeeds as long as all the teams stay on the field. But all technological competition — all innovation — consists of the pursuit of fugitive positions of monopoly....

The new information infrastructure will bring a cornucopia of new services from a variety of new sources that cannot even be defined as yet. All we know is that none of the existing rivals is likely to survive in recognizable form. Only a true freedom model that allows a complete reconstruction of the world of communications — with anyone collaborating or competing, merging or metamorphing with anyone else — can allow this new era to come to fruition. Only a freedom model can release the $2 trillion of new asset value that the scholars of restructuring promise for the U.S. economy of the 1990s and beyond.[5]

Thus, Gilder happily acknowledges that if competing telecommunications corporations are left to fight for market share without government regulation, the outcome might be a field in which only one player is left standing. But not everyone is as blithe as Gilder about the possibility of monopoly. Representative Ed Markey (D — Massachusetts) speaks of "two wires into every home" — the consumer must have a choice. If unbridled capitalism may eliminate choice, restraints are needed to prevent the tendency towards monopoly from taking its natural course. This represents the view of competition that Gilder criticizes: competition sustained through regulation to ensure that a plurality of players remain in the game.

But competition among different access providers to the inforoute may only be of the Coke-and-Pepsi variety — without seeing the bottle, most people can't tell the difference. Far more important is free choice in *content.* Does control of the transmission medium mean control of the content? If the information highway — or railway — is viewed as an extension of television, then it very well may. Historically, television broadcasters both owned the transmitters and decided what would be transmitted over them. Cablecos have operated according to a slightly different model, allowing a limited number of content providers to use their transmission facilities but generally not providing much content on their own. Telcos, on the other hand, have operated as "common carriers," providing the transmission medium — the telephone wires — but taking an essentially laissez-faire attitude towards what is transmitted over those wires.

Mergers and joint ventures among telephone companies, cable operators, software manufacturers, film producers and others suggest a convergence of transmission and content on a hitherto unimagined scale. But there are other tendencies as well: the Internet, for example, has grown up as a common carrier that carries an unprecedented variety of content — personal mail, discussion forums, online newspapers, pornographic pictures and much more. If the entities that control transmission also control content as the information highway develops, then monopoly or oligopoly can be very dangerous. On the other hand, if the information highway operates as a common carrier, then a single transmission line may make sense and attempting to duplicate it may be a waste of resources.

The Information Highway Advisory Council

Having decided in early 1994 that developing a strategy for the information highway was a government priority, Ottawa did what it usually does under such circumstances: it set a group of people to work studying the matter.

This group, the Information Highway Advisory Council (IHAC), was not the first such body. Way back in the seventies, a previous Liberal government, that of Pierre Trudeau, had appointed the Consultative Committee on the Implications of Telecommunications for Canadian Sovereignty under J.V. Clyne of MacMillan Bloedel. The Clyne Committee sought ways of managing the coming competition between telcos and cablecos and offered the kind of prediction about the new telecommunications age that would later become all too familiar: "It is not too much to say its birth is an event equal in importance to the industrial revolution of the 19th century."

But the government's actions didn't go much beyond appointing the committee. Glenn Schneider wrote in 1979:

> The federal government and its agencies have been watching this battle [between the telcos and the cablecos] shaping up with little or no action on their part, except to encourage the cable companies. While the former Liberal government [this was written during Joe Clark's brief tenure] amply demonstrated its appreciation of the dynamic nature of telecommunications,

computers and the television industry and their potential impact on Canadian society through a series of study papers, its actions to guide the future direction of policy to the greater benefit of Canadians have been minimal.[6]

Like the Clyne Committee, the Information Highway Advisory Council (IHAC) of the 1990s was strongly oriented towards private enterprise. To be sure, its twenty-nine members included representatives from academia, the cultural sector and labour as well as some appointed to ensure a degree of regional, ethnic and gender balance. The strongest voices on the council, however, were those of the major business interests involved in the inforoute: Bell, Rogers, Unitel, Vidéotron, Teleglobe and others. In its report, issued in September 1995, the council spoke the language of competitiveness, innovation, deregulation, choice and the free market. Operating under this bias, and required to balance competing interests, IHAC repeated the prevailing ideological platitudes of the day:

Canada's success on the Information Highway will depend on whether we can establish a framework for its development, one that will unleash our creativity and innovativeness. If we have the necessary foresight and boldness to push forward, then economic growth and jobs will follow.
    The most effective way we can respond is to move away from regulation and rely more on market forces.[7]

IHAC echoed the Clyne Committee's sense of the magnitude of the transformation involved, but its bland language gave the impression that it was as far from actually coming to grips with this transformation as Ottawa had been in the 1970s. Two of the three objectives set out by the government as a guide to IHAC's discussions — "creating jobs through innovation and investment in Canada" and "reinforcing Canadian sovereignty and cultural identity" — pose severe challenges that the council skipped over much too lightly (the third objective is "ensuring universal access at reasonable cost"). Instead of seriously trying to demonstrate that the information highway will serve those objectives, the council by and large simply states and assumes that it will. On the basis of the evidence so far, it can be plausibly argued that rather than reinforce Canadian sovereignty and create jobs, the information highway will do precisely the opposite.

Canada's cultural sovereignty is protected by a variety of federal policies. However, the new technologies make it possible to circumvent many of them. Electronic transmission technology made it possible for Time Warner to evade Canadian rules against split-run magazines. When Time Warner began electronically transmitting its "Canadian edition" of *Sports Illustrated* to local printing plants, it forced Ottawa to pass new legislation in the face of an intense lobbying effort. The United States challenged the legislation before the World Trade Organization, which determined that Canada had violated international trade rules. Direct-to-home satellites vastly increase the number of television channels from outside Canada that are available to Canadian viewers, making Canadian content an even more marginal part of the overall television menu than it has been in the past. Internet users received information from the United States that violated the court-imposed publication ban in the Paul Bernardo–Karla Homolka case. Material that in ink-and-paper form would be stopped by Canada Customs on obscenity grounds routinely crosses the border electronically through the World Wide Web. Large-scale electronic currency transfers make Canadian economic policies more vulnerable to international pressures.

British historian Norman Stone takes a dark view of the erosion of national sovereignty: "The modern world that was invented around 1500 is coming to an end. It was then, roughly, that the modern era came to pass: printing, law, the nation-state. Now all of that is at an end. We are back to the medieval world of beggars, plagues, conflagrations and superstitions." In our view, the picture is not quite so dismal. At least some of the developments cited above have redeeming features.

Nevertheless, we have a healthy respect for the challenge that enhanced electronic communications represent to the sovereignty of all states, including Canada. To be sure, the inforoute can be a tool for Canadians to communicate with other Canadians. But it is also, perhaps more significantly, a tool for cross-border communication, and any effort to restrict such communication as a means of promoting Canadian culture or sovereignty is increasingly likely to be futile. Federal government documents sometimes refer to "Canada's information highway" or "the Canadian information highway." These references are misleading. There is no Canadian information highway. There is an international information highway, and Canada is part of it.

The Information Highway Advisory Council paints a picture of a prosperous future filled with high-tech jobs. Undoubtedly, the information highway has already brought prosperity to some people. In 1995 we were treated to the phenomenon of the Internet stock boom — which in 1996 began to look like the Internet Bubble. After the spectacular stock market debut of Netscape Communications in August 1995, all Internet stocks were expected to rise steeply, and most fulfilled the expectation. Companies that had yet to earn a dollar in sales were valued in the hundreds of millions. A perceptive observer called it "a gold rush with no gold."

Meanwhile, for people who depended for their livelihood on employment rather than investment, prosperity wasn't quite so easy to come by. Nor was it only in the "old economy" of manufacturing and resource extraction that jobs were increasingly scarce. It was precisely in the sectors most heavily affected by the new technologies, such as banking and telecommunications, that the largest layoffs were announced. Computers, voice-mail systems and automatic teller machines replaced stenographers, receptionists, telephone operators and bank tellers. Perhaps the most disturbing trend was the breaking of the link between economic growth and employment. Throughout the supposed recovery of the mid-1990s, unemployment in Canada remained above 9 per cent. Of course the information highway creates jobs in areas like World Wide Web site design, electronic security, Internet indexing and the like. But are there as many new jobs created as there are old ones lost? And what about all the people who lose the old jobs and are not in a position to benefit from the new ones?

These and other effects of the inforoute have led a surprising number of people to declare themselves modern-day followers of General Ned Ludd, the mythical commander of the early-nineteenth-century "army of redressers" that conducted machine-smashing raids to express their opposition to the social effects of the new technology of the time. The great British historian E.P. Thompson has argued convincingly that the Luddites were not opposed to technology as such but rather to its unrestrained use by the factory owners. Similar issues are being played out in the late twentieth century.[8] While we do not count ourselves among the neo-Luddites, we believe these critics are raising questions that need to be addressed.

Ten Lies about the Highway

Marc Belanger of the Canadian Union of Public Employees, who has been active in bringing about the labour movement's own computer network, SoliNet, has outlined what he calls "ten lies the information highway construction industry is about to present to you":

1. This technology will promote education. Technology is not education, says Belanger, and it detracts from human contact between teacher and student.

2. This technology will create jobs. If this were true, in Belanger's view, the jobs would have appeared by now, and the companies that are engineering the information highway, such as Bell Canada, would not be laying off thousands of employees.

3. This technology does not destroy jobs. Nevertheless, Bell has laid off 10,000 people, Unitel (now AT&T Canada) laid off thousands, and the federal government is laying off 45,000 while buying new computer equipment.

4. There are no health and safety problems related to this technology. Computer companies initially denied problems with screen radiation as well. According to Belanger, there are health problems related to all new technology.

5. This technology enhances communities. It does provide us with certain tools for building community, but there is no guarantee that it will be used for that purpose.

6. Less body work is better for humankind. We are missing a whole lot of people in this revolution, Belanger says: people who are predisposed towards work involving the body rather than academic or high-tech work.

7. People want more entertainment. In fact, people spend hours in front of their TV sets because they are tired and stressed out.

8. This technology is better directed by private enterprise than by government. The technology was developed by government and universities, which still know more about it.

9. We know what we're doing. In fact, says Belanger, companies like Bell and its main competitors haven't a clue. They have no idea what the technology can do or what people want and need from it.

10. This is a natural step in the march towards progress in society. In Belanger's view, we're faking our way through it. It may take a whole generation before the effects of the so-called information revolution can be seen as a benefit.

Not all of these statements necessarily have to be lies. The technology can be used for education and community. Even the employment issues can be addressed, although it will take a major social effort to do so. But none of this will happen if the only guiding force in the development of the information highway is the sovereign market.

Not even Adam Smith believed as single-mindedly in the free market as some of today's zealots. Aside from protecting society from internal and external violence, Smith maintained that the state needed to be directly involved in some areas of the economy. He saw it as having "the duty of erecting and maintaining certain public works and public institutions, which can never be for the interest of any individual, or small number of individuals, to erect and maintain; because the profit could never repay the expense to any individual, nor small numbers of individuals, although it may frequently do much more than repay it to the greater society."[9] As we shall see, novel as the information highway may be in some respects, it is also only the latest in a long line of such "public works and public institutions," both in Canada and in "Adam Smith's great laboratory," the United States.

2

The Military Origins of the New Technologies

One thing the military is good at is specifying what a technology must do, like making a missile land within 30 feet or a plane fly 5,000 miles an hour.

Lester Thurow

The information highway is an extension and civilianization of the military political economy. How could it be otherwise? The satellites, launchers, space navigation computers and communications industries that make up the highway were all created by the military-industrial complex. "The same technology that produced Star Wars produced the Internet," says Ursula Franklin, "and I see the development of these things as nothing more than a continuation of the scheme that kept Star Wars going."¹ In a sense, it has always been thus. Technology has almost always been developed to serve the needs of the military and then been civilianized — from the jumbo jet to the Teflon pan. Technology and science harnessed to the military require the intervention of the state if only to appropriate the money. The development of machines — the telegraph, the railway, radio and now the Internet — has been connected with government and especially the military at least as much as with "free enterprise" or the market. The pattern holds consistently, but never before on the scale contemplated with the information highway.

Media consultant Patrick Crawley in a submission to CRTC regulatory hearings in 1993 made this point clearly:

> The original UNIX mainframe and network configurations still at the core of today's information sector ... [are] merely clones of the UNIX networks established as the space race spread the U.S. military's communications, navigation, surveillance and electronic intelligence gathering network worldwide....

U.S. military communications, navigation, surveillance and electronic intelligence gathering networks now form the proto-types for the proposed Direct Broadcast Satellite–based distri-bution sector as well as for all of the various fibre optic–based new transmission environments now being promoted by some Canadian and all American carriers.

In developing this connection, Crawley went on to describe the "new" services billed as the information revolution as "just pale shadows of systems and services which have been operational within the U.S. military networks since the '50's."

Companies that were formerly charter members of the military-industrial complex are now aggressively moving into the communi-cations field. Spar Aerospace, which designed and built the space shuttle's Canadarm, is a case in point. Spar, in its earlier incarnation as the research arm of de Havilland, was a founding member of the military-industrial complex. It has become a key element in Canada's space program as well as an important component manufacturer for the Americans. With revenues of $571 million in 1994, it is still involved in building satellites and space equipment. "But," according to the *Globe and Mail*, "it has become enamored of international communications and software. It uses satellite technology as the basis for continent-wide telephone systems, and has become inter-ested in multichannel satellite television broadcasting."[2]

The "synergy" between Spar's new CEO, Colin Watson, and Spar, which moved into space communications several years ago as the traditional defence contracts began to shrink, is clear. When he was the president of Rogers Cablesystems, Watson was also a director of something called Canadian Satellite Communications Inc., which delivers television signals by satellite to cable companies and pro-vides satellite communications services to business.

Watson's move from Rogers to Spar seems to indicate that mili-tary technology and the civilian communications technology in the information highway are part of the same seamless web. But there are complications, and they are related to the circumstance that the inforoute is being built in a new world freed from the discipline imposed by the Cold War. These complications affect Canada and contribute to the crisis in our evolving regulatory system.

The State and Public Enterprise

In fostering the development of the information highway, the state, and primarily the American state, has gone far beyond regulating and controlling the market. As in previous periods of rapid technological change, it has created, orchestrated and financed the technological revolution reflected in the new global economy and the information highway. From railways, telegraph and telephone communications in the nineteenth century to satellite transmissions and computer technologies in the late twentieth, the state has played a central role in the development of new technologies. To appreciate the function the state has fulfilled and needs to fulfil in creating and developing the information highway, it will be helpful to take a brief look at the historical interplay among communications technology, military considerations, and the Canadian and U.S. governments.

We have plenty of examples of the state's role in the development of new technologies in Canada. Even the CBC was created by two impulses — the desire for a public broadcasting system as well as the more mundane need to bail out the bankrupt Canadian Marconi Company. The government's industrial mastermind, C.D. Howe, was much more interested in salvaging and promoting the hardware than in public broadcasting itself. If it could have been done by private capital, Howe would have been quite happy. Similarly, he had tried to interest private capital in a national airline with or without government partnership before proceeding with Trans-Canada Air Lines by incorporating it into the crown-owned Canadian National Railways. This pattern of government leadership of the market in new technology development, whether by intention or by default, is repeated throughout the direct and indirect military sphere, from Polysar and the petrochemical industry to Canadair, Spar and the high-tech infrastructure stretching from Montreal and Ottawa into southern Ontario.

A similar pattern holds true in every developed country, including the United States. Economist Lester Thurow credits American defence spending (and so, by extension, the American state) with ensuring the crucial lead held by the United States in the technologies of software, hardware, the Internet and biotechnology. The last half century has given North America enormous power and substantial technological superiority. Through the requirements of the Second World War, the subsequent arms race and other military adventures from Korea through the Middle East to Vietnam, the American state

was able to organize, finance and develop the technological infrastructure of the information highway. U.S. commercial, industrial
and financial interests have been able to use this advantage as the
new millennium approaches. The continuation of the American technological advantage as the military-industrial complex is civilianized
is reflected in a study by Morgan Stanley: between 1987 and 1992,
U.S. corporations captured 47.7 per cent of global profits and 37.4
per cent of global sales. With American production expanding and
Japan and Europe showing less vigorous growth, it is safe to assume
that this advantage is widening.

The current merger mania is closely related to the onrush of the
information highway, and thus to the changing priorities of the
American state. A 1995 article in the *Wall Street Journal* noted that
the whole defence industry was ripe for consolidation and added that
then–defense secretary William Perry appeared to be encouraging
such rationalization.[3] He "came from industry and understands business concepts," an analyst was quoted as saying. The same article
also noted that "U.S. Vice President Al Gore's vision of a nation-
wide information superhighway is advanced by mergers among giant
communications companies." To encourage this process the U.S
government relaxed its antitrust guidelines, and by the time Perry
resigned at the end of President Clinton's first term, the American
defence industry had seen Boeing's takeover (presented as a merger)
of McDonnell-Douglas, and Raytheon's purchase of Texas Instruments for US$2.95 billion and within two weeks its US$9.5 billion
purchase of the Hughes Electronics division of General Motors. All
of this left the other major Pentagon supplier, Northrup Corporation,
which has spent more than US$5 billion on acquisitions since 1994,
as a mere "niche player."

Canada and the U.S. Military Economy:
The Beginnings

Canada has played a central role in the creation, development and
expansion of the American military economy. The failure of the
American invasions of 1775 and 1812, and Canada's subsequent
political independence, did not prevent the northern half of North
America from becoming integrated into a continental defence
scheme. In the 1920s the Americans reluctantly — and then not so
reluctantly — agreed that Canadian political independence had its
positive features. A politically independent Canada served American

interests well in Suez in the late 1950s, in the Turkish–Greek conflict in Cyprus and of course in Vietnam. Canada, in spite of any romantic illusions to the contrary, has always been part of a continental military, economic and diplomatic structure.

As the world entered the age of modern industrial and increasingly technological war, defence agreements naturally broadened into the areas of technology, industry, transportation and communications. For example, we began building the trans-Canada highway system in the early 1920s much along the lines of, and in the spirit of, the transcontinental railway. While the east–west railway system has lost its dominant position and one could argue that the trans-Canada highway has yet to be completed, Canada's modern highway system is designed in no small measure to link our major urban centres with the American Interstate system, which was financed and built under the aegis of the Pentagon. Our railway system seems to be following suit, for as lines are abandoned in whole sections of the country, Canadian National and Canadian Pacific have both spent massively to acquire or build new links with U.S. railways.

Canada's position within the American defence system was formalized at the onset of the Second World War. In a speech at Queen's University in 1938, President Roosevelt recognized Canada as part of the British Empire then sliding into war with Germany. "I give you my assurance," he said, "that the people of the United States will not stand idly by if the domination of Canadian soil is threatened by another empire." When Canadians attached great importance to this remark, Roosevelt was astonished. "What I said was so obvious," Roosevelt noted.[4]

Later, in the face of the Blitzkrieg, he and Prime Minister Mackenzie King signed the Ogdensburg Defence Agreement in 1940 and the much more important Hyde Park Declaration several months later. What was always "so obvious" to the Americans was that North America was indivisible and that Canada was under the protection of the United States. And in addition to being obvious, it was now also operational in that joint defence agreements were to be buttressed with defence production sharing agreements.

Although as early as the 1930s the United States was Canada's most important trading partner and capital market, in a very real sense these defence sharing agreements anticipated the full economic integration of Canada into the American system. The treaties reflected the fact that Canada was now effectively part of the United States. Britain was to be the third-party recipient of military and economic aid from a "Greater America," and it was to pay dearly for this aid. This process, manifested in the various extensions of military production as well as operational integrations from NORAD to cruise missile testing, continued through the whole period of the Cold War.

Canada and the U.S. Military Economy: The Cold War

The core of the agreements between Canada and the United States was defence production sharing. This assumed one dimension during the war but a very different one afterwards when Britain was more or less excluded — without warning President Truman cancelled the Lend Lease agreements and reneged on a previous commitment to share atomic data. Canada, meanwhile, had signed contracts to sell uranium exclusively to the United States. The postwar tripartite alliance of English-speaking nations was mostly illusory. The United States viewed Britain as a rival and it viewed Canada as part of its domestic affairs; the Suez crisis showed that Canada essentially accepted this way of looking at things.

The American economic boom of the early postwar years also brought prosperity to the vast resource hinterland, Canada. Canada's portion of military procurement boomed as well, so that it contributed to and benefited directly from North America's great technological advantage. In a strict sense Canada never fully got its share of North American military spending. But how does one draw a strict line that excludes Canada's energy and natural resources from the American military machine?

The postwar reconstruction was civilian only in part. The manufacturing and technological lead that the role of bankroller and chief military supplier gave the United States was shared in Canada through its universities, research institutions and independent and branch-plant manufacturing facilities converted to the war effort. Canada's aircraft assembly plants, which began operating in the 1920s and were easily converted to military production, constituted an early example. During the war, when no private facility existed, crown corporations were created, and after the war these were sold or virtually given away to private, often American, concerns. Apart from the transfer of ownership, the facilities and jobs remained in Canada and thus allowed Canadians to keep up and develop their military expertise.

In retrospect it is not only what Canada made during and after the war that is of significance but also what it was able to do with what it made. British military historian Ronald Lewin has stated that every large war has its salient characteristics, and if the unprecedented use of masses of artillery was the most striking feature of the First World War, signal intelligence — SIGNIT — was the dominant feature of the Second World War. Walter Laqueur writes: "Since then enormous technical progress has been made in SIGNIT technology with its main components of COMINT (radio communications intelligence), ELINT (the interception of electronic signals) and RADINT (radar intelligence)."[5] Canada participated in these components — the basic structure of the inforoute — from the beginning.

Canada's enthusiasm for the Cold War was certainly ideological; it was also seen as good business. In 1951 the government pledged $5 billion over the following three years, and by the mid-fifties more than 40 per cent of the federal budget was being spent on defence.

Economic integration with the United States began to take concrete form with the Defence Production Sharing Agreements in the late 1950s. Commentators have made the point that Canada's share of joint defence production was usually in low-tech areas — we manufactured the green berets. However, some of the most sophisticated guidance and communications systems were made at least partially in Canada. Ernie Regehr's definitive study *Arms Canada* contains several pages of appendices listing Canadian companies that manufacture switchgear, microcircuits and other sophisticated components for the American military.[6]

Canada was the third country in space, but it still does not have the capability of launching a rocket. Its military integration into the United States is exactly like its total economic integration: it makes components. Vital components, sophisticated components, but components nonetheless.

Following a pattern of economic integration as old as John A. Macdonald's National Policy, American communications, computer and aeronautical giants set up shop in Canada. What began during the Second World War continued apace as C.D. Howe organized Canada's postwar reconstruction. Litton Systems, MacDonald Dettwiler and Spar joined other major "Canadian" players in the military-industrial complex — General Motors, Ford, Chrysler, General Electric and Westinghouse. Robert Reich writes: "Throughout the 1950's and 1960's, 100 core corporations, (mostly involved in aerospace and telecommunications) received two-thirds, by value, of all defense contracts. Ten firms received one third."[7] All of the ten and most of the hundred have facilities in Canada. Many of their operations in Canada would likely fall under American appropriations.

Partly because of its geographical position as the land mass that stood between the continental U.S. and the USSR, Canada developed a particular expertise in electronic communication. In *Target Nation,* James Littleton notes the growing importance of Canada in American strategic military planning. This importance took shape in the 1950s in the form of bases leased to the United States for the Strategic Air Command through membership in NORAD and the development of warning systems from the Pinetree Line to the considerably more advanced Distant Early Warning (DEW) Line.

The DEW Line was a vast system of radar stations reaching across the Canadian Arctic from Alaska to Greenland, but it was also much more. As Littleton points out, "Not many systems could be more complex than a system intended to defend a seven-million-square-mile continent from intrusion by one, ten, or a hundred aircraft approaching at various speeds, altitudes, directions, and headings." Thus the DEW Line meant the construction of several thousand interceptor aircraft, the manufacture of nuclear warheads and "the development of sophisticated mechanisms for the integrated command and control of all these forces."[8]

Canada spent $320 million on the DEW Line. The project provided thousands of jobs and transferred important technology into Canadian hands. It also serves as a prime example of when and how our peculiar partnership with the United States developed. One of the major contractors on the DEW Line was Northern Electric, from which Northern Telecom (now Nortel) emerged as Canada's electronic communications giant. In the 1950s Northern was the manufacturing arm of Bell Canada, which was closely associated with AT&T (Northern had access to the patents of Bell Laboratories in the United States until 1975). Thus the line between Canadian and American technological development is blurred. Indeed, while the DEW Line was on Canadian territory, the United States was responsible for security. When a press tour of the facility was organized in 1956, Canadian reporters had to fly to New York, then agree to have their copy censored by American authorities, then pass American security tests and accept American travel authorization — to visit their own country.[9]

There is one exception to Canada's role as component manufacturer, an exception that proves the rule. During the Second World War, an agreement was struck between Britain and the United States that had Britain concentrating on the development of fighter aircraft while the Americans developed bomber and transport planes. The British firm A.V. Roe had a plant in Canada, and during the war Hawker Siddeley built an assembly plant in what is now Thunder Bay. The Roe plant, through several incarnations, continued to develop fighter aircraft, and finally built the complete Avro Arrow in the 1950s. The Americans refused to buy the Arrow, and Canada could not afford to go it alone. As they say, the rest is history. The old Roe complex became part of McDonnell-Douglas and then Boeing which, as branch plants, make components. It is now owned by Bombardier through Canadair.

From the Cold War to the Information Highway

The Cold War created a discipline in which all American allies suppressed their national interests in the battle against Communism. While this discipline came unravelled from time to time, on the whole the alliance held. But "alliance" does not quite capture the nature of the relationship; rather, the Cold War worked towards turning all the countries of the West, and for that matter the East, into American satellites — military, economic and cultural. In relation to Canada, John Sloan Dickey has written:

> The Cold War ... seemed to most observers in Canada as well as the United States to be the first external security threat to North America in modern times. The threat was perceived as inescapably common to both countries, one which could only be countered by the closest military collaboration in an unprecedented peace alliance. During this period of "continentalism" in new defense arrangements, there was a rapid expansion of the American cultural and economic presence. American publications and broadcasting became overwhelmingly dominant in the mass media, and American direct investment, freshly stimulated by Labrador iron and Alberta oil and gas, became so pervasive in Canada that it could not long go unnoticed and unresented.[10]

How much it was resented is of course a subject of debate. But that nothing was done to reverse the trend or even slow it down is obvious. Canada has not merely worked with, but has actually been an integral part of, the development of the U.S. military-industrial complex. The Canadian government has been part of this creation just as the American government has. And we have always stuck to our role as component manufacturers.

The same tangled relationship between Canada and the United States extends to the civilian arm of the communications industry. Bell Canada, along with its subsidiary Northern Telecom, began life as part of the AT&T monopoly. In the mid-1950s Northern Electric, as it was then called, made its living supplying telephone equipment to Bell Canada, which owned 56 per cent of the company. It got almost all its technology from Western Electric, the manufacturing subsidiary of AT&T, which owned the other 44 per cent. However, a complicated 1956 consent decree, proceeding out of an abortive attempt undertaken during the Truman administration to force AT&T to divest itself of Western, led to Northern's being cut loose from its American parent and becoming a wholly owned subsidiary of Bell Canada. Northern also now had to develop its own designs.

In the 1970s Northern, which did not operate under the same regulatory constraints as Bell Canada proper, became its parent's chief vehicle in Bell's move to transform itself from a staid old telephone company into a leader in the new world of telecommunications. Renamed Northern Telecom, it began opening manufacturing plants outside Canada and seeking international markets while cutting jobs at its Canadian plants. It was encouraged in this direction by the regulatory agency of the time, the Canadian Transport Commission, which hoped that increased profits from Northern would allow Bell to moderate its insistent rate increases. In its new guise as a telecommunications multinational, Northern Telecom became a shining star of Canada's policy of promoting technological innovation.[11]

As of 1997, AT&T has returned to Canada to try to break Bell's monopoly. Canadian AT&T president Jim Meenan has said, "I know what monopoly power is and it's ugly." AT&T wants back into the old local services, which now include new services ranging from wireless to Internet access. To get around Canadian laws, which for the moment restrict foreign ownership, AT&T has entered into equity partnerships, marketing arrangements and licences with various Canadian firms including three of Canada's major banks. AT&T has always considered Canada (in its own words) "part of our domestic market," and a significant part at that. According to Meenan, "There are more minutes of use that leave the United States and go to Canada than any other country in the world."[12]

Any claim Canada would have to its own military-industrial complex could only be based on its companies' role as parts suppliers for the Americans. Yet, partly because of geographical considerations, partly because of the high level of communication technology in Canada, and partly because its main technological, communication and industrial base was already American-controlled, Canada played a rather extensive role in developing this technology. "Within [Canada's] defence industry," wrote Alistair D. Edgar and David G. Haglund in their 1995 study of the industry, "the major areas of strength are in aerospace, electronics, and communications, where there exists some capability for total systems-design integration. This capacity, however, requires considerable technical and financial support and this can be obtained or developed most easily by the subsidiaries of larger foreign companies."[13]

As the components of the defence system transform themselves in the United States into the components of the information highway, it seems increasingly unlikely that Canada will have an inforoute of its own. Canadians are being required to think increasingly in continental terms. However, we are not starting from point zero, nor is our problem simply a matter of playing catch-up with the more powerful and advanced economy to the south as was the case with railways, radio and television. In other words, close association with the United States has not always worked to Canada's disadvantage.

Big Brother: Friend or Foe?

Spare a thought for George Orwell and *1984*. Things didn't quite work out the way Orwell predicted. To be sure, we now have the ubiquitous "interactive" telescreen over which Big Brother can watch us, and revisionist histories and biographies can be published instantaneously over the information highway Orwell foresaw in a cruder and more limited form. However, instead of perpetual war and shifting alliances among three power blocs, one of the blocs — the United States — emerged triumphant.

But the essential inaccuracy in Orwell's prophecy is Big Brother himself, which Orwell envisioned as the totalitarian state with its control over all history, communication, culture and entertainment.

Rather than the state controlling us, it is private corporations that alienate our culture and make us strangers to one another in our own land. For Canada, the issue is complicated by the fact that English Canada is part of the larger American continental economy and culture and yet at the same time distinct from it, with its own interests. We have our own corporate sector, which wants nothing more than a piece of the action. Thus it often stands against the public interest and must be regulated by some public body. The issue therefore is not so much Big Brother as getting Big Brother involved and on our side.

The American state, as the instrument of American capital interests, is moving strongly to develop, control and regulate all major aspects and manifestations of the information highway. It means to bring order to the North American system and, in fact, to set the rules for the universal network.

In all likelihood it will be unable to do this. This incapacity does not mean the United States is not the biggest and most technologically advanced society — it is in all respects the world's only superpower. Rather, the skein of issues and the implications and possibilities of global communications networks go beyond the scope of jurisdiction of the traditional single nation-state, no matter how big and powerful it may be when compared to its rivals.

In fact, the issues raised are somewhat analogous to those in the old Law of the Sea conundrum, where such questions as pollution, the food chain, climate and undersea and ocean-bed exploitation broke the traditional compromises of freedom of the seas and territorial limits that had been operative since Britain ruled the waves. Like the debates over the Law of the Sea, the coming issues of the information highway don't involve ideology — at the Law of the Sea conferences the Soviets and the Americans were usually allies — but rather the universal problem of an old order unable to adapt to or cope with, much less contain, a new technological regime.

Documents issued at the Law of the Sea conferences always included formulations like "the oceans as a common heritage of mankind." Now we see the emergence of a Commission on Global Governance, with a manifesto entitled *Our Global Neighborhood*. Whether any global regime can be established is, however, problematic. In the meantime, the outcome of the American state's efforts to control internal development and reassert its dominance universally is crucial for a country like Canada.

Within that context, there is a limited but nevertheless real set of increasingly obvious and viable protective steps that Canada can take. In the first place we must agree that we are part of a single North American communications system. There will be no parallel east-west system like the old railways. Yet within this single grid Canada can insist that there are (to coin a phrase) distinct societies, and it can act on this premise by creating both a regulatory role for government and a proactive screen for Canadian cultural interests as well as an impetus towards building a modern technological infrastructure.

3

The Growing Corporate Empires

We have already mentioned the inadequacy of the term "information highway" as a metaphor to describe the various phenomena that have been emerging or converging over the last few years, lumping together aspects of technology and content that had no apparent links until quite recently.

Richard Schultz, a long-time analyst of the telecommunications and broadcasting industries and a McGill University professor of "political science fiction," as he sometimes likes to call his chosen academic field, is one among many writers who have pleaded for a halt to use of the term "information highway":

> The problem is not simply ... that there is far too much hype associated with the concept. From my perspective the problem is even more serious.... As a metaphor, it is far too constraining, too encumbered. It conjures up, as [Robert] Fulford argues, "something with a clear direction."
>
> Secondly, as an analogy, I dislike the term "information highway" because it may give rise to the impression that traditional thinking, traditional policy responses, traditional policy makers, are appropriate. When I think of highways, I think not simply of concrete and pavement but of engineers. And engineers, physical and especially social, are the last people we should let near the information policy sector.[1]

Before we grapple with the weighty question of whether engineers — or, perhaps more ominously, bankers, securities dealers and conglomerators — should determine how information and entertainment are to be disseminated, we have another quibble with the highway as metaphor.

Highways, again, suggest clear directions and fixed paths. The telephone lines that have adorned the landscape for more than a century and the coaxial cables that bring television signals into millions of homes quite evidently follow fixed paths, but not even the owners of these links can say with any certainty how this will shape public or commercial policy directions even a short time into the future. Broadcast signals and cellular telephone systems, on the other hand, do not follow fixed paths: although they rely on fixed infrastructure, they cover their territories like blankets rather than snaking out like bands of concrete.

Railways, with their archaic, nineteenth-century aura, may seem even less likely than highways as metaphors for the cornucopia of transmissions that seem destined to come at us from as yet unimagined directions as we enter the twenty-first century, but in Canada anyway there are strong historical analogies.

In his book *Wire Wars,* Toronto *Globe and Mail* reporter Lawrence Surtees recounts that the Bell Telephone Company of Canada and the Canadian Pacific Railway Company were created only ten months apart in the early 1880s. After a brief period of competition, the two companies proceeded to establish dominant positions in the telephone and telegraph fields, respectively, keeping a gentlemanly distance from each other's domains. At the time, it was not at all clear that the telephone would emerge as the dominant medium. This truce was broken more than a century later with Canadian Pacific's efforts to enter the long-distance telephone market through its holding in CNCP Telecommunications (later renamed Unitel, later renamed AT&T Canada). But meanwhile Bell and Canadian Pacific had much in common:

> Their inception ... occurred at the hands of the same corporate lawyer and the same government, which also saw fit to grant them almost identical powers in communications. Both companies hired Americans to carry them through their infancy as they each struggled to forge sweeping monopolies in their respective fields. As different as telephones and trains are, their businesses greatly resemble each other — they move things on highways of wire or steel and both enterprises are critical to the economic fortunes of the nation.[2]

Another thing telephone and railway companies have in common is their fierce and jealous control over the rights-of-way they own.

Railway companies in Canada and the United States will happily convey freight cars belonging to other companies over their tracks, but only in trains they operate themselves. They are willing to allow passenger trains operated by the likes of Amtrak or Via Rail to run along their tracks if the price is right, and they even agree reluctantly, under special circumstances, to accord running rights over limited portions of track to rival freight-hauling railways. But traditionally they have quivered with wrath at suggestions that their tracks and other infrastructure should be open to other companies, even if these companies accept stringent conditions relating to fees, schedules and so forth. Heaven forbid that competition should break out along these sacred rights-of-way!

Nowadays these attitudes are starting to soften. Canada's two railway giants, Canadian National and Canadian Pacific, talk occasionally of consolidating their networks east of Winnipeg to squeeze out excess capacity and reduce unit operating costs. In theory, this could allow them to recapture some lost business from truckers, although a more likely outcome, given the resulting absence of competition within the railway industry, would be just the opposite. But what if, instead, they allowed other operating companies, including those without an inch of mainline track they could call their own, to run freight trains using this allegedly excess capacity, in competition with the owners of these rights-of-way?

This concept is not much more revolutionary than the idea of rival truckers sharing the same highways, but it has stirred howls of outrage among railway executives, at least until recently. It seemed not to occur to them that the flexibility and innovation new operators could bring might actually reverse the long-term decline in their industry's share of freight haulage, as some short-line operators have proven. Though this may stretch beyond the ken of traditionalists, the day may not be all that distant when the operation of trains becomes separate from the ownership and maintenance of rights-of-way. This, after all, is how it has always been with highways. Governments (or, in rare cases, private firms) build and maintain the road network, but vehicles using this network are owned and run by individuals or commercial operators quite separate from the road owners.

Telephone companies have behaved in much the same way as the railways. Over more than a century, they have made the enormous and continuing capital investment required to link millions of homes and businesses with their ever-growing networks, they have built huge customer bases (with a lot of help, obviously, from the statutory monopolies they continue to enjoy), and they will be damned if anyone they regard as an interloper is going to have access to all of this. Or at least that was their attitude until long after the process of deregulation was set in motion in the United States during the presidency of Jimmy Carter. The purpose of this exercise, which is still far from complete, was to replace government regulation with competition. For there to be competition, the dominant and tentacular American Telephone and Telegraph Company, more commonly known as AT&T or by a variety of sometimes unflattering nicknames, had to be carved into pieces. This was done in the early 1980s with the creation of seven regional Baby Bells, each providing local service within set geographic boundaries, and with AT&T reincarnated as a long-distance carrier only.

Canada's monopoly telephone companies, and most particularly Bell Canada, far and away the biggest of the lot, were not impressed by what was happening south of the border, and they fought tooth and nail to prevent any interlopers from gaining even limited access to *their* infrastructure and *their* customers. This was a battle they eventually lost, but not until after their legendary and breathtaking arrogance had been thoroughly exposed. It took some time, but Americans and, a few years later, Canadians began to get used to the idea of long-distance telephone competition. Only in 1996 did the United States begin moving towards competition in local telephone service and in cable television service. Canada followed suit a year later.

Canadian telephone companies, and their relatively weak siblings in the cable television industry, still resist the notion that anyone besides themselves should derive much benefit from the infrastructure they have built so painstakingly. In this, of course, they resemble the railway companies rather than highway owners.

In fact, vertical integration in the communications and information industries goes even further than it does in the railway business. Both the railway and highway models allow for a distinction between service and content. While Canadian Pacific may operate nearly all the trains that run over its lines, it does not control what shippers put into the freight cars or containers that make up these trains except to regulate weight and hazardous substances. The owners of highways (usually meaning governments) establish criteria as to the types of vehicles that may use these highways, but again they do not control what moves in these vehicles except where weight or safety are concerned.

Similarly, telephone companies offer communications services but generally refrain from providing or controlling the content of what moves over their lines, their recent entry into Internet services notwithstanding. In the broadcasting and cable industries, on the other hand, licence-holders exert direct control over the content of what is transmitted. Broadcasters nearly always have to face competition, even in remote areas. Cable operators, on the other hand, usually enjoy local monopolies, the rationale being that they have to be compensated for their heavy investments in infrastructure. They can determine in large measure what their customers may see and hear through the selection of channels they offer as part of both their basic and extra-rate services, as well as their arbitrary powers over so-called community access channels. Before the Internet became dominant, providers of online computer service exerted many choices on their customers' behalf, and still do now, although to a far lesser extent. Commercial online services such as America Online and CompuServe were initially characterized by integration on three levels: ownership of infrastructure, service over this infrastructure, and control over the content of this service.

But it is not difficult to envisage a time when the company that owns the infrastructure ceases to be the service provider over this infrastructure, renting it out instead to separate and competing operating companies. Only then will we be able to speak of an information highway rather than an information railway. In their book *The Medium and the Muse*, telecommunications whiz kid Charles Sirois, currently chair of Teleglobe Inc., and public policy analyst Claude Forget, a former Quebec cabinet minister, argue strongly against vertical integration in the communications and information industries, insisting that provision of infrastructure and provision of services should be split and handled by separate entities. They say different service providers should be allowed to compete freely using a common infrastructure. In other words, they prefer the highway model to the railway model.

The dangers of vertical integration, Sirois and Forget argue, can be seen clearly in the film industry, dominated as it is by the big Hollywood studios. With the huge distribution costs they face, the Hollywood majors are not content merely to keep the whip hand over film production in the globally dominant American industry. They also insist on extending this same domination to film distribution in

North America and, to a lesser degree, in Europe. Thus MCA sub-sidiary Universal Studios controls Cineplex Odeon, Columbia Pictures owns Sony Theaters, Paramount is linked to sister company National Amusements and owns Famous Players, Warner Brothers and Paramount together own Cinamerica Theaters, and MGM owns United Artists Theaters.[3]

These companies together own many thousands of screens and account for a giant share of film exhibition in the United States and Canada. And the film majors exert considerable control even over the chains and independent cinemas they do not own themselves. They do this, for instance, by requiring multiscreen cinemas that want access to box office hits to turn over their other screens to films that may have won little critical or commercial acclaim. Since there exist only a finite number of cinema screens, independent producers and distributors have a difficult time getting their films exhibited, particularly if these films are not produced by Americans. Foreign films are thus mostly shut out of the U.S. market, with the exception of a few small art houses in big cities and college towns.

Hollywood honchos portray their wares as commercial rather than cultural products that should not face any entry barriers to foreign markets, but they exercise a monstrously powerful form of protectionism over their enormous home market. In 1993, U.S. film exports totalled $2.53 billion, while imports came to a measly $85 million.[4] This nearly 30-to-1 ratio results from the industry's control over the means of distribution rather than any perceived inferiority of foreign films or even the proverbial parochialism of American audiences.

Imitating the United States would not be a sensible answer for Canada. Breaking the direct vertical links between film production and film distribution may, on the other hand, offer at least part of the solution, as unpleasant as this may be for the Hollywood majors. It could help break down industry cartels and give moviegoers a broader choice. It could also make it easier for filmmakers in Canada and elsewhere to raise money and reduce reliance on arbitrary tax-supported schemes aimed at promoting or protecting bureaucratic notions of what constitutes national culture.

The film industry is probably an extreme example of what is wrong, and of what can go wrong, if vertical integration is allowed to prevail in the communications, information and entertainment industries. But this does not diminish its value as a warning. What good is an information highway, or an information railway, if the metaphoric trucks or freight trains moving along it are filled with force-fed junk?

Sirois and Forget hold views that run counter to orthodox notions of what constitutes Canadian nationalism, but they argue that the U.S. model of vertical integration on the inforoute must be stopped at the Canadian border. The Canadian market is too small to allow for competition between vertically integrated giants. U.S.-based companies that happen to be vertically integrated should not be blocked from investing in Canada, but they have to decide which hat they want to wear in Canada. Since these same restrictions would apply to Canadian companies (and MCA is controlled by the Seagram Company, which has its nominal head office in Montreal), they should be able to pass muster with trade authorities.

Vertical integration restricts consumer choice, raises entry barriers to particular industrial sectors, and reduces competition in places where it is most needed to encourage growth and development. Canadian producers of content and applications, Sirois and Forget go on to argue, have what they need to compete on the world inforoute, but they require the support of public policy that stimulates their spirit of enterprise and opposes commercial protectionism at home or abroad.[5]

Do these arguments reek of neoliberal twaddle, or can they provide useful elements for a made-in-Canada formulation of cultural and commercial policies? Where Sirois and Forget diverge from many other defenders of market forces and supporters of free trade is in their insistence that government has a role to play in the development of the inforoute, even if this role consists mostly of setting conditions that allow for lower barriers to new entrants and freer competition.

Monopoly and Competition

Monopolies are easy to hate. Either they are rich and powerful, like the traditional phone companies, or they are incompetent and arrogant, like Canada Post, or they combine all of these characteristics, like some cable TV companies. And yet, when we look at the other side of the coin, we have to wonder if competition is all it is cracked up to be. Canadians have become accustomed to, and sometimes even fond of, certain monopolies. The CBC held a monopoly on television broadcasting during much of the 1950s; the programming Canadians see today is slicker and more varied, but do people really like it better? In most provinces, Canadians get cheap, reliable electricity from monopoly suppliers. Long-distance telephone rates are perhaps higher than they should be, and this in a field now open to competition; local telephone service remains a monopoly, and most users are reasonably satisfied. Do we really want more competition, with the stresses it imposes on workers and managers alike, its depressing effects on wages and job security, and its war-of-all-against-all ethos?

The answer is a qualified yes. Monopoly and its close cousin oligopoly often lead to unearned privilege and immovable complacency among those who hold the reins. One need not look as far as the former Eastern Bloc countries to see the effects that the absence of commercial competition can have on living standards. It is simply better to have choices. There have even been exceptional cases, right here in Canada, where the absence of competition has meant no service at all. This was our embarrassing experience in 1995 and 1996 in the domain of direct-to-home satellite television, after the CRTC set conditions that effectively prevented anyone from competing head-to-head with ExpressVu, the spectacularly incompetent outfit that received the first licence to bring Canada into the much ballyhooed 500-channel universe but failed to deliver anything. More on this in Chapter 5.

Competition has its harmful side, but it can, and often does, bring lower prices, better service, greater variety and increased innovation. One does not have to be a political Neanderthal to acknowledge this. The question is how to promote competition while attenuating its negative effects. Canada, as usual, lies somewhere between the United States and western Europe in areas such as labour protection and social safety nets. The United States tends to be weak in these areas, but this very weakness has spawned flexible labour markets and high rates of job creation at varied wage levels. Europe imposes greater obligations on employers and provides workers with generous benefits, but many European countries suffer from unemployment rates that are even higher than those in Canada.

Whatever the advantages of competition, certain industries were long considered suitable only for monopoly status because of the enormous cost of providing the necessary infrastructure. This was especially true in the area of public utilities, where it simply would not pay to have more than one set of water mains or electricity transmission lines or streetcar tracks. Even today, not even the most ardent advocates of privatization and competition would have an easy economic argument to make if they sought to justify duplication in any of these areas.

The field of communications has been much the same. The railway companies built telegraph lines alongside their tracks and enjoyed local or regional monopolies in many places. When Canadian National and Canadian Pacific merged their telegraph operations, this became a national monopoly, albeit in a declining technology that got its last gasp from Telex operations and from the share of data transmission CNCP managed to hold onto after squandering the jump it had briefly gained over the telephone companies. Having stayed off each other's turf for many decades, the telegraph and telephone companies did not have highly developed competitive instincts. The telephone companies were licensed to operate monopolies in both local and long-distance service across entire regions, a situation that changed only in 1991 with the introduction of long-distance competition.

Economists and public policy analysts have struggled mightily to come up with answers to the monopoly-versus-competition conundrum, and we do not pretend to have any magic solutions. What we *can* do is to observe that competition is increasingly international in scope and that this has dented what some would call complacency — and what others would call basic security — among workers in Canada and other high-wage countries. Ending globalization, however, would create as many problems as it would solve: it would favour greedy local oligopolists over more efficient or innovative producers and would take away, in the form of higher prices, whatever gains workers could win in wages and benefits. And it would be devastating for workers in export-oriented industries in low-wage countries. The idea of international worker solidarity, based loosely on the Marxist concept of proletarian internationalism, has evoked only faint whispers and has a long way to go. Still, it holds more promise than rearguard actions fought within national boundaries when it comes to tilting the balance in the global struggle between labour and capital.

Until recently, the service sector has been less exposed to international competition than manufacturing. You may buy a shirt made in Thailand or India, but you're not going to call a plumber over from Asia to come fix your toilet in Canada. Some areas of the service sector, though, are becoming more global. Only official restrictions on foreign ownership and control prevent powerful groups in the financial services industry from operating unhindered in any country they like, helping preserve, for instance, Canada's banking oligopoly. The same applies to the airline industry. Broadcasters, on the other hand, have long had to cope with cross-border competition, while in telecommunications the fun has just begun. U.S. giants such as AT&T and Sprint have established a highly visible presence in Canada and several other countries, while international call-back services are making it harder for monopoly providers to maintain egregiously high rates.

One result of increased competition has been heavy layoffs at old-line phone companies such as Bell Canada and even at newer ones such as Unitel (renamed AT&T Canada). On the other hand, the telecommunications sector as a whole has grown quickly, creating job opportunities elsewhere. Another result of competition is higher local phone rates, balanced by lower long-distance rates. This is likely to work against poorer people, who tend to make fewer long-distance calls. One solution is to reduce the level of vertical integration — in other words, separate the services carried over monopoly networks such as the basic telephone system from the ownership of these networks and open service provision to competitors in return for fees. The company that builds and maintains a network should not be allowed to retain monopoly control of it. Access to it should be open to anyone who is qualified, as with highways, rather than restricted, as with railways. This change would bring competition in price and service for local calls as well as for long distance. The same separation between network ownership and service provision should apply to cable TV, ending the monopoly abuse so many consumers have complained about.

Providers of cable television services, with their heavy investment in coaxial cable, cling jealously to their local monopolies and dismiss any suggestion that others should be allowed to compete with them. Meanwhile, they argue that they should be allowed to expand into areas the phone companies regard as falling within their own realm, such as long-distance services. Rogers Communications won that argument in the hearing rooms of the CRTC with its investment in Unitel, but then lost the battle in the real world when a failed business strategy forced it to write off its investment.

The phone companies have ambitions of their own, of course. With their hefty capital resources, they could swallow the cable companies for breakfast if only the CRTC and the federal cabinet would step aside. Broadcasters, who do actually have to face competition, also have ideas as to who should be allowed into what field and at what cost. Everybody in the communications industry in Canada wants to be allowed onto everybody else's turf, it seems, but nobody appears willing to cede an iota of precious inherited privilege.

The same is true in the United States, where the Federal Communications Commission (FCC), roughly equivalent to the CRTC, is regularly deluged with missives from firms in every known sector of the communications industry. Michael Katz, the chief economist of the FCC, was quoted on this theme in a 1995 article in the *New Yorker*:

> TV broadcasters say, "We want free markets, but we don't believe that the government should use markets to sell us spectrum." TV broadcasters have their own definition of a free market — "Give it to us free and we'll market it." Radio broadcasters say they favor free markets, but they ask the commission to block competition from entrepreneurs who want to use satellites to deliver radio services. The local telephone companies say, "Get out of our way and let us into the video-dial-tone business." Then you say to them, "How about letting the electrical utilities into telecommuncations?" They say, "Don't let them in!" The cable companies say, "Don't let either of them in; they'll use their captive-monopoly rate bases to compete unfairly." Yet they want no pricing regulations for themselves. The long-distance telephone companies say we should let them into the local telephone business, but they don't want the local companies in the long-distance business. So all industries say, "Get out of our way — but regulate our rivals."[6]

The Rogers Empire

If this greed, envy and confusion about who should be allowed to do what — and under what sort of regulatory protection — were limited only to the sorts of communications companies that fit the traditional mould of what we used to think of as public utilities, things would be relatively simple. In response to changing commercial and technological environments, there would still be some sorting out to do between companies in the public sector and those in the private sector, those that face competition and those that have statutory monopolies, those that operate in more than one domain, and so on. But instead, the term "information highway" has acquired a broader meaning that leads to the even more nebulous concepts of multimedia and convergence.

Many industries — local, long-distance and cellular telephone companies, cable television companies and their emerging satellite-to-home competitors, broadcasters, publishers, film studios, online services and Internet providers, developers of computer hardware and software, makers of consumer electronic goods, and other sectors also — have engaged in frenzies of mergers, diversifications, take-overs and multilateral alliances as they chase the ephemeron of global multimedia dominance. Some deals have worked well; others have been abysmal failures.

Things have not always moved this quickly. Look at how long it took Canadian Pacific to get back into the telephone business after its failed experiment between 1888 and 1891 with the Federal Telephone Company, when rate reductions induced by competition between Federal and Bell led to huge losses and a humiliating withdrawal. This was an almost eerie harbinger of what Canadian Pacific would suffer with Unitel just a little over a century later.

In *Wire Wars*, Lawrence Surtees recounts in great detail the many years of intense lobbying and the numerous setbacks that Canadian Pacific had to endure before the CRTC finally relented in 1991 and allowed CNCP Telecommunications (renamed Unitel the year before) to enter the long-distance telephone market in competition with the Stentor alliance, dominated by Montreal-based BCE Inc. and its biggest operating subsidiary, Bell Canada. Canadian Pacific, after buying out Canadian National and becoming sole shareholder in CNCP Telecommunications, had sold a 40 per cent share to Rogers Communications and its domineering supremo, Ted Rogers, Jr., in 1989. Despite his minority stake, Rogers was named chair of CNCP, with Canadian Pacific apparently content to play second fiddle. The key reason for this was not hard to fathom. As Surtees writes:

The view on the street was that Rogers was given that licence in the partnership because of his unprecedented political access to the government of Brian Mulroney. The former chairman of the Youth for Diefenbaker organization, nicknamed "Rogers' Raiders," had cultivated that access since December 1956 when Mulroney, then a keen seventeen-year-old student, approached Rogers to volunteer his services at the Tory leadership convention. Rogers introduced the St. Francis Xavier student to a senior Diefenbaker strategist who proclaimed Mulroney a vice-chairman of the youth organization. Rogers hoped to have the favour returned with the long-distance bid.[7]

Rogers had been only five years old when his father died. Ted Rogers, Sr., was heir to a family fortune, developer of a system allowing radios to operate from household current rather than batteries, and founder of Toronto radio station CFRB (the last two letters stand for Rogers Batteryless).[8] Ted, Jr., heir to a now bigger family fortune, would perfect the art of manipulating regulatory and political authorities, a talent far more valuable in the cable TV industry and the other regulated fields Rogers Communications has entered than any ability to run an efficient or innovative business.

Minority shareholders in Rogers Communications have had to show the patience of Job as they suffer through the ambitious expansion plans of the company's mercurial chair, chief executive and major owner. Ted Rogers, Jr., has loaded the company with staggering debts to build what he says will be Canada's first major multimedia empire. The biggest gulp to date has been the 1994 takeover of Maclean Hunter and its extensive cable TV and publishing assets for $3.1 billion. The financial performance of Rogers Communications has been anything but reassuring, with losses totalling $283,357,000 in 1995 and $278,370,000 in 1996. Losses have been swollen by interest charges on the company debt and by a 1995 writedown of $152,607,000 to get out from under the grossly mismanaged Unitel, which in 1993 was accumulating losses at an average rate of $1.5 million per day and was still hemorrhaging badly when Rogers and Canadian Pacific unloaded it onto a consortium made up of American communications giant AT&T and Unitel's major Canadian creditor banks.

Ted Rogers told shareholders at the 1996 annual meeting that losses would continue for several years to come. Building a multimedia empire is not cheap, even in a market as small as Canada and even when backed by cash-cow revenues from the country's biggest cable TV operations, with profits almost guaranteed by monopoly status. The Maclean Hunter takeover, added to existing assets, brought Rogers control of about one-third of all cable TV operations in Canada and more than two-thirds in the Ontario market.

The company has not grown big by endearing itself to customers. One particularly egregious gaffe was its 1995 attempt at negative-option billing, whereby customers were saddled with costly new services automatically unless they took action to prevent it. Book clubs and other mail order outfits have practised something comparable for decades, but at least they tell their customers up front what to expect. Even Rogers had to admit this billing ploy was a mistake. Nor did Rogers make friends in Vancouver with its attempt in 1994 to block use of fibre optic cable installed within the Pacific Place condominium development that could distribute television signals at substantially less cost than Rogers customers were paying.

Ted Rogers is the Canadian personification of the industries Michael Katz describes as saying, "Get out of our way — but regulate our rivals." In taking over Maclean Hunter, Rogers argued that his stranglehold on the Ontario cable TV market would allow for a coordinated defence against the "deathstar" satellite and the phone companies. But a few years earlier, as he sought to enter the long-distance telephone market that had been all but monopolized by Bell Canada and its Stentor partners, Rogers had promised, in words of breathtaking hypocrisy, to end the phone companies' "Soviet-style communications monopolism."[9] Rogers has never been shy about attacking monopolies other than his own.

All cable TV companies, of course, protect their monopoly positions, to the eternal unhappiness of many customers. Toronto-based Rogers happens to be the biggest and most powerful cable TV company in Canada, making it an easier target than most others. Montreal-based Vidéotron was set to capture the number-two spot with its 1996 asset swap with CFCF Inc. that would give Vidéotron control of the cable assets of both companies; meanwhile CFCF would consolidate the two firms' broadcasting operations, including all three of Montreal's private-sector television stations. This deal, which was delayed by lawsuits on behalf of jilted suitor Cogeco Inc., will push Calgary-based Shaw Communications into the number-three spot overall, although without weakening its powerful position in western Canada.

For most cable TV customers, the degree of concentration hardly matters, for in any given town or urban neighbourhood a particular firm is going to have a monopoly anyway. If rates and service are reasonable, it makes little difference whether this firm has operations in numerous other localities. Thus, for example, Montreal Island has been divided in two up to now, with Vidéotron holding the cable TV monopoly on the eastern half of the island and CF Cable serving the west. Customers cannot choose between these two companies: the CRTC has already done it for them. When these two companies become one, the level of choice will not be any different: it will remain at zero.

Heavy concentration can have the effect of making innovation less likely. The more firms there are, the more likely it is that at least some of them will seek novel ways to cut rates or broaden service. Vidéotron, for example, has experimented long before most other cable companies with interactive services and devised plans for a sophisticated online venture that could link many homes that have no computers. Rogers, in contrast, has been more of a laggard in pursuing innovation.

What Rogers is attempting to do is build a multimedia empire, based around cable TV with content coming in part from the various newspapers, consumer magazines, trade publications and data services that it obtained in the Maclean Hunter takeover. Crushed by debt, however, Rogers in 1996 divested some of these assets, including the Toronto *Sun* and its sister newspapers in three other cities. A multimedia strategy is not without its obstacles.

For both Rogers and Canadian Pacific, the Unitel gamble may have seemed less risky when they set out to convert sleepy old CNCP Telecommunications into a new-age long-distance phone company. This effort, begun long before Rogers became involved, required literally decades of lobbying before the CRTC and the federal cabinet, opposed every inch of the way by Bell Canada, which was not about to give up even a smidgen of its lucrative monopoly powers without a fight. CNCP's first major victory against Bell came in 1979 when the CRTC granted CNCP, then a telegraph and telex company that had made successful forays into the fast-growing data transmission field, the right to interconnect with phone company lines. But Bell and its fellow phone companies still retained their hugely profitable long-distance monopolies, and they managed to rebuff a 1983 effort by CNCP to get into that business. It was not until 1991, following an even more acrimonious battle, that Bell and its allies finally suffered defeat in a closely watched series of CRTC hearings, ushering in long-distance telephone competition in Canada.

"I haven't changed my mind about it. Competition and regulation cannot live side by side in any industry," former Bell chief Jean de Grandpré had said in a 1990 interview with Lawrence Surtees.[10] But de Grandpré's successors at Bell would show that this sluggish old beast could in fact learn to compete despite its age-old status as a cosseted monopoly. Indeed, the agility shown by Bell and some of the other old-line phone companies in their pricing and marketing policies may have caught Unitel by surprise, depriving it of the extra-high growth rates it needed to support its bloated structures.

De Grandpré had converted Bell Canada into a subsidiary of a newly created conglomerate named BCE Inc. that ventured with varying degrees of accomplishment into fields as varied as pipelines (more or less a success) and commercial real estate (a dismal flop). After his retirement, BCE narrowed its focus, concentrating on the telecommunications field and retaining its majority ownership in Northern Telecom (now Nortel). Although BCE suffered a blow when Bell lost its long-distance monopoly, it gave up none of its appetite for domination. In 1992 BCE acquired control of two companies previously owned by the federal government, Teleglobe Canada (the monopoly provider of overseas links, which the CRTC had awarded a few years earlier to tiny Memotec Data) and Telesat Canada (the monopoly satellite operator). BCE also tried to muscle its way into a quasi-monopoly of direct-to-home satellite TV through its partnership in ExpressVu, which was also going to use BCE-owned satellites. To put it gently, ExpressVu has not been among corporate Canada's great achievers (see Chapter 5).

Multimedia Mergers

The multimedia frenzy in the United States seems only to be starting, with levels of vertical integration that reach for the sky. On the last business day of 1995, the business section of the *Los Angeles Times*, which often seems as infatuated with Hollywood as the entertainment section of that same newspaper, ran a feature article titled "Hollywood's Wildest Ride":

> To say that 1995 was the wildest ride for the entertainment business in decades would be no understatement [*sic*].
>
> Never in such a concentrated period has there been such cataclysmic activity in this crazy place called Hollywood.
>
> A liquor company bought a studio. A major studio and a big industrial company each acquired a broadcast network. A media giant merged with a leading cable programmer. And some of the last independent movie companies lost their independence or simply disappeared....
>
> At year-end, $40 billion in mergers had been transacted and more than $200 million in severance packages went out to those who lost their jobs.

If there was one mantra among media moguls this year, it was that bigger is better. Global distribution operations have insatiable appetites for movies and TV shows. That makes content more valuable and makes global conglomerates like Time Warner Inc. and Walt Disney Co. eager to have more. The trick is to find novel ways to repackage existing products to keep distribution channels humming, offset rising production costs, and add to revenue and leverage potential.[11]

Here is a partial list of the deals that went through in 1995 (all amounts are in U.S. dollars). In March, "Microsoft Corp. co-founder Paul Allen invests $500 million in DreamWorks SKG, bringing the capitalization of the studio formed by Steven Spielberg, Jeffrey Katzenberg and David Geffen to more than $2 billion. Microsoft later becomes a smaller investor." In April, "Seagram Co. signs a deal to buy 80% of MCA Inc. from Matsushita Electric Industrial Co. for $5.7 billion." In May, "MCI Communications Corp. agrees to invest $2 billion in Rupert Murdoch's News Corp." In July, "Walt Disney Co. bids $19 billion to buy Capital Cities/ABC Inc." In August, "Westinghouse Electric Corp. bids $5.4 billion to buy ailing CBS Inc." In September, "Time Warner Inc. announces plans to merge with Turner Broadcasting System Inc. for about $7.4 billion in stock, a deal that would reaffirm Time Warner as the world's biggest entertainment conglomerate." And in November, "Barry Diller takes control of Home Shopping Network and Savoy Pictures. Westinghouse takes control of CBS."[12] An interesting year indeed.

If 1995 was a busy year for mergers and buyouts in the entertainment and information industries, 1996 was just as busy in the communications industry, following Congressional approval on February 1 of a law allowing companies in the local telephone, long-distance telephone, cable and broadcasting industries to enter one another's turf. This came a decade and a half after AT&T, long the overwhelming giant in the telephone industry, was broken up to form the dominant U.S. long-distance carrier, which kept the AT&T name, and seven regional companies referred to collectively as Baby Bells.

In 1996, the map was about to change again. AT&T, after announcing plans to get rid of its money-losing NCR Corp. computer division and also to spin off its research-oriented Lucent Technologies division, said it was preparing to jump back into the local telephone business. Two of the Baby Bells, California-based Pacific Telesis and Texas-based Southwestern Bell (which had adopted the natty initials SBC), announced plans for a merger. They were to be followed to the altar by Bell Atlantic and NYNEX, which between them serve most of the northeastern United States. NYNEX also announced a deal to sell long-distance services over Sprint lines, while U.S. West said it would take over Continental Cablevision in a $10.8 billion deal.

Bigger is better, the mantra goes, but things don't always work the way they are planned. For instance, the Seagram Company, under the stewardship of Edgar Bronfman, Jr., was looking for something more glamorous to invest in than the chemical industry and decided to tender its sizable Du Pont holding, buying 80 per cent of MCA with the proceeds. MCA is the parent company of Universal Studios, the ownership of which had been a very painful experience for Matsushita, the Japanese consumer electronics firm better known under its Panasonic and National brand names. Whoever had whispered nonsense about synergies from vertical integration into the ears of top Matsushita bosses was proved wrong by the multibillion-dollar bath the company suffered. It turned out there were no synergies to be found in playing videos released by Universal Studios on Panasonic VCRs. (Sony Corp. fared little better with its takeover of Columbia Pictures and Columbia Records, although it decided to stay in for the long haul.)

We hear the word *convergence* time and again; the term *multimedia* seems to crop up just as frequently. Both have a technical meaning, but when they are carried into the domain of corporate organization they express the vague notion that there is some enormous advantage to be gained by bringing telephone service, cable, broadcasting, film and TV production, publishing, computer software, theme parks and so on under the same umbrella. Time Warner, Disney, and Rupert Murdoch's News Corp. (which includes Fox television and the 20th Century Fox film library) are just some of the more obvious examples of multimedia empires. They are being joined by telephone and cable companies that want a taste of the glamour.

Quite apart from actual mergers and buyouts, there has been a steady and incestuous dance of alliances in which a small number of well-known players seem to be working the permutations. Thus we read in 1993 that U.S. West, one of the Baby Bells, was preparing to invest $2.5 billion for a stake in Time Warner, with particular interest in an experimental interactive video network. At about the same time, Viacom and AT&T were working on a similar deal. Neither got very far. Later that year, NYNEX invested $1.2 billion in Viacom to back Viacom's takeover of Paramount Communications. Meanwhile, Bell Atlantic announced a $32 billion takeover of John Malone's Tele-Communications Inc. (TCI), the biggest cable operator in the U.S., but this deal collapsed, as did a $4.9 billion cable television partnership between Southwestern Bell and Cox Enterprises.

In 1994, Sprint Corp., TCI, Cox and Comcast formed a joint venture to bid on wireless licences across the United States and to provide a broad package of services via cable. Not to be left out of the action, Microsoft announced a raft of deals in 1995 and early 1996, including a joint venture with DreamWorks SKG to develop interactive entertainment products, a deal with General Electric–owned NBC for a twenty-four-hour news channel, and an arrangement with MCI Communications to sell each other's products and services. In a further deal, Microsoft joined in an alliance with MCI and Digital Equipment Corp. to develop corporate data networks called intranets, going head to head against a similar alliance formed by AT&T, IBM and Netscape Communications. Another 1995 deal involved MCI investing up to $2 billion in Murdoch's News Corp. to deliver News Corp. content over MCI lines. Meanwhile, News Corp. was preparing to invest hundreds of millions in a joint venture with MCI to provide satellite television services. Described somewhat patronizingly by *The Economist* as "the most interesting media tycoon in the world," the Australian-born Murdoch had to become an American citizen to catch the deregulation wave of the Republican Congress and expand his American empire. Murdoch has also set his sights on capturing the Berlusconi interests in Italy, as well as building his satellite system in Asia.

Nobody can be content with a piece of the action, everyone wants all of it — yet nobody has a clear view of where the action is and where it is developing. There will one day be an industry standard and a monopoly. And many of today's technological wonders will go the way of the Stanley Steamer and — in a modern analogy to the turbine versus the internal combustion engine — who can say that the superior systems or technologies will always win out?

Lewis J. Lapham describes the present corporate feeding frenzy over control of the information highway and compares it with the earlier railway boom:

At least twice a week for the last several months, the newspapers have been bringing word of yet another massive deal in
progress among the gargantuan media syndicates, and always
the breathless prose implies exclamation points: Murdoch Ac-
quires Rights to Asia! Viacom Bids 10 Billion for Paramount!
Pygmies Flee! Giants Walk the Earth.... I think of the furious
building of railroads that excited the American imagination
during the last decades of the nineteenth century.[13]

Lapham goes on to make connections between the current atmosphere and the one that characterized the railway boom. There are
several elements that connect. In each era there is a struggle by the
new modes to supersede such "intermediate technologies" as the
stagecoach in the nineteenth century or the rooftop antenna and the
copper cable in the late twentieth. But the main thrust of the frenzy
is control — monopoly. Lapham continues:

The words "us" and "control" allied [John] Malone with Com-
modore Vanderbilt and John D. Rockefeller, both of whom
knew that the rules of finance capital decreed remorseless com-
bat between the triumphant few (us) and the hapless many
(them), and that the amassing of great wealth presupposed
absolute command of the means of transportation.[14]

It is perhaps worthwhile noting that the emergence of the fabled
robber barons of the late nineteenth century brought forth the antitrust and antimonopoly legislation of the early twentieth century in
the United States. These measures are now widely seen as ineffec-
tual, archaic and even counterproductive — they merely led to internal trusts such as General Motors, spurious divisions such as the
various Standard Oils and rather dubious judicial outcomes such as
the splitting of the Bell monopoly, the action against IBM and the
threats against Microsoft. For example, the American government
successfully scared away Microsoft's $2 billion takeover of a soft-
ware rival because it would give Microsoft almost exclusive control
over the emerging financial services artery on the highway. And then
IBM moved on Microsoft's competitor Lotus Development for precisely the same reasons. Harking back to the bad old days before any
regulation, a White House staffer began referring to Microsoft's Bill
Gates as "the Jay Gould of the information age."

The Dangers of Vertical Integration

Most corporate publicists extol the virtues of competition. With deregulation, companies can step more freely onto their rivals' turf, but that still doesn't mean they like others stepping onto their own turf. An item in the *Wall Street Journal* mentioned that Ameritech, the Chicago-based Baby Bell, had taken measures making it harder for many customers to switch to other providers of local service. Meanwhile, U.S. West had pulled a manoeuvre to protect its Centrex office-phone business, AT&T was pushing federal regulators to bar the Baby Bells from sharing customer data with long-distance services they operate outside their home regions, and Home Box Office, a division of Time Warner, was refusing to provide programming to Ameritech for its new cable systems. In the words of a communications consultant quoted in the article, "Everybody's eager for competition — in everybody else's market."[15]

The increased competiton that ought logically to result from the 1996 U.S. communications law ought just as logically to bring lower rates to cable television subscribers in the United States, but the contrary has occurred. For instance, TCI, the biggest cable operator, announced a 13 per cent across-the-board rate increase for June 1996. Cable operators said they needed higher rates to recover from rate cuts imposed in 1993 "after a consumer backlash that prompted Congress to reregulate the industry," a *New York Times* article noted. "What makes this wave of increases remarkable is that it comes even before cable rates are to be deregulated yet again," in 1999 under the terms of a congressional compromise.[16]

There are lessons here for Canada in two areas: in multimedia deal-making and in moves towards reduced regulation of the communications industry. Canada, with its small number of big players, simply does not offer the same possibilities for deal-making as the United States does, although the influence and direct interests of American companies in Canada can often mean that the Americans are doing the deals for us. As national barriers and regulatory frameworks erode under the pressures of economic ideology and technological change, it is becoming easier for American and other non-Canadian firms to buy, merge or affiliate with companies in Canada. The most obvious example of this up to now has been AT&T's effective takeover of Unitel in partnership with the Canadian banks that were Unitel's creditors. With its minority stake, AT&T has secured management control of the newly named AT&T

Canada, presenting an interesting conundrum for the regulatory authorities that are supposed to uphold rules stipulating that Canadian telecommunications companies must stay in Canadian hands.

Another case in point is Fonorola, a Montreal-based long distance reseller that leases facilities from other carriers at wholesale prices and then resells them to individual customers. Fonorola has signed a partnership agreement with Canadian National to use the railway company's 33,000-km right-of-way to expand and improve CN's fibre optic lines. This became somewhat more complicated when Fonorola entered a partnership with New York–based Chase Manhattan bank in an attempt to compete with AT&T Canada and Stentor. In 1995 Fonorola executed a share swap with Teleglobe that enabled it to take over the smaller Optinet Communications. A holding company controlled by Lord Jacob Rothschild owns more than one-third of Fonorola. We currently have laws in Canada that are supposed to limit foreign ownership in the telecommunication sector to 20 per cent. But these regulations — always open for amendment — are honoured mostly in the breach.

The Canadians who are supposed to own at least 80 per cent of telecommunications companies can include corporate entities that in turn are at least 80 per cent Canadian-owned. Eighty per cent of 80 per cent equals 64 per cent, which means that foreign interests can quite legally hold up to 36 per cent ownership rather than the 20 per cent that the regulations appear at first glance to suggest. And this does not take account of nonvoting shares or of the fact that even a relatively small holding can provide effective control if the remaining shares are widely enough dispersed or if service contracts give command over important aspects of operations. Thus the 20 per cent benchmark can be quite meaningless. Let's take an example from the airline industry, where regulations allow foreign interests to hold up to 25 per cent of voting shares. In the so-called partnership between American Airlines and Canadian Airlines, the vastly larger American Airlines abides by the 25 per cent rule, but it controls scheduling, maintenance, the all-important reservations system and ticket pricing. In other words, it controls Canadian Airlines.

The issue is much more complex in the tangled ownership structure of the telecommunications industry in the aftermath of the American court decision to break the telephone monopoly in the 1980s and create the Baby Bells. There is in North America one communications system operated by several managements. Moreover, the antitrust decisions may have forced the creation of several different corporations and managements but it didn't alter the system's ownership. The people and institutions who owned AT&T before its recent spinoffs, and still own it, are the same people and institutions who owned it as a monopoly. They also own all the Baby Bells in America. This ownership structure spills over into Canada through Unitel, now AT&T Canada. A likely eventuality is that if AT&T can't stay within the 20 per cent limit, the rules will be changed or else — considering the precedent of the federal decision declaring Seagram a "Canadian company" — redefined.

Even within the Canadian playpen, we see at least a limited amount of deal-making as well as moves by communications companies to move onto one another's turf. Thus, for instance, we saw Bell Canada and IBM move towards a deal under which IBM would take over the computer operations of the Bell Sygma subsidiary and Bell would provide network services to IBM's Advantis subsidiary.[17] Rogers has encroached on telephone company turf through its Cantel cellular operation and its ill-fated investment in Unitel, all the while insisting that the phone companies should stay away from cable. Rogers has also sought to build a multimedia empire incorporating the publishing assets acquired in the Maclean Hunter takeover, and it is a minor partner in a venture between Microsoft and TCI. Without film libraries or sizable television production assets, however, Rogers is still rather weak on the content side, at least compared to the giants it seeks to imitate such as Time Warner, News Corp. or Germany's Bertelsmann. Meanwhile, Bell keeps making noises about entering the cable field and is working through its MediaLinx subsidiary to develop content for a future online network.

The headlong rush in the United States to multimedia empires and alliances, with communications companies grabbing exclusive access to important chunks of content, will probably serve the public interest less satisfactorily than what might occur under relatively open arrangements that could put the word *free* into free markets. But the United States is a big country. Even within the oligopolistic framework of the big communications and media enterprises, there is enough competition to avoid the spectre of monopoly control of entire industries. Canada is a smaller country, with a more tightly knit oligopoly, and the prospect of real alternatives and real choices is less certain. Multimedia empires just won't work in the Canadian context, except for the managers and shareholders of the favoured companies. The only way to avoid stifling dominance by a tiny handful of companies would be to throw open our borders to foreign competitors, some of whom could digest the entire Canadian market with barely a burp. Goodbye to any notion of cultural affirmation.

In the separate but related matter of breaking down the barriers that have set tight limits on intrusions by communications companies onto one another's turf, it seems to be only a matter of time before Bell and its sister telephone companies, with their solid balance sheets and their strong revenue flows, get the green light to swallow the cable industry. This is not all bad, as long as certain conditions are met.

The most important of these conditions is a prohibition on vertical integration. Vertical integration can lock in valuable assets in the form of film libraries, television production studios, and other sources of content, and keep them out of competitors' hands. These assets — at the moment primarily film libraries — may generate less revenue than they would if their products could be sold to the highest bidder, and it means everyone's sources of entertainment and even information will be more limited. It also raises the barriers to entry that new firms face at various points along this ever-longer vertical chain, meaning less innovation and variety in the future.

Ideally, a prohibition on vertical integration should mean not only that providers of basic communications service should act as conduits for content providers rather than being in the business of providing the content themselves, but also that owners of infrastructure such as telephone and cable networks should not even be providing service along these networks. Instead, these networks should be treated as public utilities, open to all qualified service providers in return for suitable fees.

We have seen how highways, which are open to virtually anyone with a suitable vehicle, have captured dominant shares of passenger and freight traffic from the railways, with their monopoly control over their lines. The communications industry can learn from this. A true information highway, open to all, can serve Canadians better than the information railway we have now. It will be cheaper, more flexible, more competitive and more responsive to local interests.

4

The Internet

While telcos, cablecos, entertainment conglomerates, computer companies and government regulators positioned themselves to become
players in the sophisticated information highway of the future, the
rough-and-ready but already existing proto-highway, the Internet,
began to capture the imagination of the public — especially that
portion of the public that was young, technologically with-it and
male. In its year-end issue, *Newsweek* proclaimed 1995 "the year of
the Internet":

> Can you recall a day when there *wasn't* some gee-whiz Internet
> story in the newspapers? Was there ever a time when surfing
> was performed in a bathing suit, outdoors? When advertise-
> ments on buses did not emblazon a string of puzzling letters
> beginning with HTTP:// and getting weirder from there? When
> Java meant coffee, and showbiz insiders used the term Web to
> refer to a saurian entity known as a television network? When
> you didn't know how to verbally articulate the @ sign? If you
> strain, perhaps you can remember such a time — 1994.[1]

Even Ann Landers's column has been increasingly given over to
letters from people reporting their Internet experiences, ranging from
"A Netizen from Chicago" who fell in love with a Canadian woman
he met on the Net, to "Older but Wiser in Bakersfield, Calif.," who
"succumbed to the lure of electronic intimacy on-line" and "wound
up being raped and nearly strangled to death."[2]

An Internet connection, generally obtained either through an institutional affiliation such as a university or large corporation or
through a commercial Internet service provider (ISP), provides the
user with a variety of resources: electronic mail, the opportunity to
participate in thousands of discussion forums known as "newsgroups," and a number of gateways (the most popular being the
World Wide Web) that provide public access to information stored

in computers around the world. The boundaries of the Internet are fluid; according to one description, "If a network accepts the teachings of the Internet, is connected to it, and considers itself part of it, then it is part of the Internet."[3]

This thoroughly postmodern grab-bag is of mixed parentage, and perhaps its most unlikely forebear is the Pentagon, which in the late 1960s and 1970s through its Advanced Research Projects Agency (ARPA) financed a pioneer computer network called ARPANET that eventually developed into the Internet. The packet-switching technology that ARPANET adopted was based on RAND Corporation research into decentralizing military communication systems so that they could survive a nuclear war. In the 1990s, this same decentralization has helped make the Internet resistant to corporate or government control. Furthermore, because of the experimental nature of computer networks at the time, ARPA ended up funding researchers whose goals had little in common with those of the Pentagon. Howard Rheingold, one of the chief boosters of the revolutionary potential of computer networks, describes the process:

> The essential elements of what became the Net were created by people who believed in, wanted, and therefore invented ways of using computers to amplify human thinking and communication. And many of them wanted to provide it to as many people as possible, at the lowest possible cost. Driven by the excitement of creating their own special subculture below the crust of the mass-media mainstream, they worked with what was at hand. Again and again, the most important parts of the Net piggybacked on technologies that were created for very different purposes.[4]

The network of networks to which the ARPA researchers gave birth expanded to include a wider community of scientists and other researchers, mostly based in universities, government agencies and large corporations. In the 1990s it spilled beyond these institutions as Internet connections became available at modest prices to virtually anyone with a home computer (including the present writers) through local Internet providers and commercial services such as CompuServe, America Online and Prodigy. It also expanded beyond North America to include other parts of the world, although North America still accounts for a disproportionate number of users of the

Internet and English remains its common language — sometimes even in newsgroups dealing with non-English-speaking cultures.

An estimate of thirty million Internet users worldwide circulated widely in late 1994. It was based on a figure of 3.22 million computer sites connected and an estimate of ten people per site. Others challenged the calculation and especially the number of people per site. Calculations of the number of Canadians on the Internet have been even more speculative. Concluding his review of the figures in a posting to the can.infohighway newsgroup, Roy Brander wrote at the beginning of 1995, "My guess (that word is *GUESS*): At least 1 million, maybe 1.5 million. So there you have it, for whatever it is worth. That is, not much." Perhaps the only safe statement is that however many people in Canada and elsewhere were on the Internet in late 1994, there are significantly more in early 1997. A March 1997 Nielsen survey estimated the number of Internet users in North America at more than fifty million — 23 per cent of the population over the age of sixteen.

With all its growth, the Internet retains the characteristics that make it very different from the corporate vision of the information highway. It still has no central authority, is primarily a medium for many-to-many communication rather than passive entertainment, is anarchic in culture and is largely noncommercial. "The corporate sector has been slow to latch onto the Internet because they can't get a handle on it," said David Sutherland of National Capital Freenet in Ottawa in 1995. "There's no Internet Inc. You have to think of it as air, and they can't deal with that." For a long time, promoters of the corporate information highway dismissed the Internet as low-bandwidth, merely a carrier of text, and therefore not worth worrying about.

In 1994, however, a new face of the Internet began to emerge with the growth of the World Wide Web. Initially developed in Switzerland in the late 1980s as a means for physicists to communicate with one another, the Web has one feature that separates it from other Internet resources: "hypertext links" that allow a user to move easily from a highlighted word to a document providing further information about that word. Nevertheless, the Web remained a relatively obscure part of the Net until the mid-1990s, when the advent of new "Web browsers" such as Mosaic and later Netscape enhanced its graphic and multimedia capabilities and made it more accessible to users. "This craze for the Internet," wrote software engineer Ellen Ullman in 1996, "[has] become a frenzy because of the Web.... The Web is turning the net into television — TV for the ostensibly intelligent. It may not be acceptable to say that you have been up all night roaming through the high, weird channels on the cable. But somehow it's fine, impressive even, to say that you clicked around for ten hours on the Web."[5]

The combination of hypertext links and high-quality graphics has made the Web the preferred location for online magazines, commercial sites, advertising and visual experiences such as virtual tours of the Louvre or the Sistine Chapel. With the rapid expansion of the Web, the Internet is growing in slickness and technical sophistication and coming closer to fulfilling the notion that most people have of the inforoute. In November 1995 Rogers Cablesystems began marketing its Rogers Wave system, which uses a cable modem some seventeen times as fast as the fastest telephone modem then in general use. The increasing speed of electronic communications, which reduces annoying delays in gaining access to detailed visual images and film clips, further amplifies the potential of the Web.

For its more ardent proponents, the Internet represents possibilities that are far more radical, and more beneficial, than those embodied in the highway imagined in corporate boardrooms. "Get wired," headlined Toronto's *Eye* magazine in March 1994. "The information superhighway is corporate crap, but the Internet is not."[6] An information highway based on the Internet offers a considerably more attractive prospect than one based on cable television. The Internet grew up outside the control of large corporations, is genuinely interactive, and breaks down barriers of nationality, gender, age and institutional affiliation, among other hierarchical constructs.

Of course there are skeptics as well, including those who are not shy about calling themselves "neo-Luddites." In the August 1995 issue of *Harper's*, two prominent skeptics, Sven Birkerts and Mark Slouka, squared off against two of the leading Internet proponents, John Perry Barlow and Kevin Kelly:

KELLY: If you hung out on-line, you'd find out that the language is not, in fact, flattening; it's flourishing. At this point in history, most of the evolution, most of the richness in language, is happening in this space that we are creating. It's not happening in novels....

SLOUKA: But there *is* a real decline in the kind of discourse taking place. I go back to what John said in an interview that I read not too long ago. He said that the Internet is "CB radio, only typing." That really stuck in my mind, because there's an incredible shallowness to most on-line communication. I realize that there are good things being done on the net, but by and large the medium seems to encourage quickness over depth, and rapid response over reflection.[7]

We count ourselves among the proponents, albeit with reservations. While it should be clear from the overall tone of this book that we are far from being techno-utopians, we do believe that there is some substance to the claims being made about the possibilities that lie in computer networks. In a society where communication has historically been one-way, the simple "Reply" button, allowing someone who has read an article on an Internet newsgroup or World Wide Web site to post a response that will then be available to all subsequent readers, has revolutionary potential. Our reservations lie less in the potential of the medium itself than in the prospects of that potential being realized. The advent of a particular technology does not necessarily lead to a specific kind of social change. There is still much to be said about who controls the technology, the specifics of its design and the uses to which it is put.

According to Rheingold, people who have been given access to computer networks have, by and large, opted to use them for communicating with one another — sometimes to an extent that has surprised and dismayed the networks' developers. When France's Minitel system was introduced in the 1980s, for example, the popularity of its *messageries* or chat services far outstripped expectations.

To be sure, much of the chat was about sex, as it often is on computer networks. It is not uncommon for newcomers to computer discussion groups, whether Minitel *messageries* or Internet newsgroups, to quickly become frustrated by the mountains of inanity they have to wade through to find anything worthwhile. Nevertheless, the popularity of what Rheingold calls "CMC" — computer-mediated communication — is at least an indication that people want more than passive entertainment or home shopping opportunities. They want to be able to talk back. Anyone reading an article in an Internet newsgroup can post an immediate reply that has the same distribution as the original article. Setting up one's own Web site is slightly more difficult. By contrast, people seeking access to older media are generally restricted to ghettos such as the letters to the editor page or the community-access cable channel, and even access to these ghettos is subject to decisions by the owners of the media. It is in giving people the tools to talk back that the inforoute has the potential for being something other than an expensive toy or a mechanism for corporations to increase their output while decreasing their workforce.

Today's Internet may represent a window between military domination and commercial domination. Will the democratic-anarchist element of the information highway be able to survive in parallel with the corporate-commercial element that will inevitably be a major part of it? The Internet has often been compared to the "Wild West," in the sense that it sprang up in advance of social organization: people simply staked their own territory. Eventually the land was surveyed and authority was imposed, although the early west left a significant mark on American culture. The Internet now appears to be at that transitional stage. The culture of the early Internet may well be marginalized as the information highway develops, but it is not likely to be completely obliterated.

A Commercial or Noncommercial Medium?

There is a prevailing belief that the Internet is hostile to commercialism, and the grain of truth supporting this belief is that one of the major features of Internet culture is a strong resistance to certain forms of advertising. It is acceptable to publicize a product or service on a newsgroup that relates directly to that product or service. Online versions of magazines and home pages on the World Wide Web contain advertising. But commercial e-mail and mass distribution to large numbers of newsgroups have been met with fierce resistance. Thus, Grant Waldram of Melbourne, Australia, who closes all his postings to the Internet with the message, "I BOYCOTT ANY COMPANY WHO USES MASS ADVERTISING ON THE INTERNET," is giving voice to a widespread sentiment.

The best-known case of mass advertising is that of Arizona lawyers Laurence Canter and Martha Siegel, who posted an ad for their immigration law practice to every newsgroup on the Internet. They were punished for this infraction with a barrage of "flames" (vituperative verbal attacks), which grew to the point where their Internet service provider could no longer handle the volume and cancelled their account. Similarly, Michael Seidel, vice-president of sales and marketing for a small computer company, underwent an intense flame attack after posting 3,000 unsolicited e-mail ads.

Canter, Siegel and Seidel all remained defiant, but it has become clear that saturation methods are not the most effective ones for online advertising, at least as things stand now. "The Internet is becoming a business network," wrote Jim Carroll, coauthor of the *Canadian Internet Handbook*, in a posting to the can.infohighway newsgroup on January 3, 1995, "used by businesses, for the purpose of making a profit.... [Internet participants] recognize this to be reality, but everyone is ensuring that it won't happen in an unacceptable fashion (hence, Canter & Siegel methods will *never* be successful)."

Similarly, Michael Strangelove, author of *How to Advertise on the Internet*, writes that online advertisers can succeed only if they adapt to Internet culture. He identifies a broad array of Internet marketing tools: establishing your own conference, distributing free documents or online newsletters, using classified ads, creating "malls" and "storefronts" on the World Wide Web where customers can find images and descriptions of products along with information making it easy to place an order, and the like.[8] All of these methods have been used without causing the negative reaction elicited by Canter-and-Siegel-style "spamming." Nevertheless, at the front of his book, Strangelove cites several hostile comments culled from the Internet on the very idea of a book promoting online advertising.

The point is not that the Internet is inherently noncommercial, but that it follows a different model of commercialism from the usual point of comparison, television. A television commercial is beamed at viewers whether they want to see it or not, often to viewers' great annoyance even though by this time, in North America at least, most people have become accustomed to the idea that the program they are watching will be periodically interrupted for a sales pitch. Online advertising bears a closer resemblance to advertising in a newspaper or magazine, where the reader at least has the choice of whether or not to read an ad. It is interesting to note that this same distinction was made in the early 1920s by U.S. Commerce Secretary Herbert Hoover in rejecting the improbable notion that radio broadcasting, at that time still the domain of hobbyists, would ever be paid for through commercial advertising. The subsequent history of radio and later television represents a cautionary note to the assertion that the Internet will never be commercialized.

In the burgeoning but still somewhat experimental world of online newspapers and magazines, the search for effective advertising formats and approaches is active and ongoing. In April 1995, a visitor to the home page of *Hotwired*, the online version of *Wired* magazine, would find an ad for General Motors' Saturn car in a corner of the page. Clicking onto the ad, the visitor is offered a variety of choices, one of which is to order a Saturn brochure. In ordering this brochure, the visitor supplies information — age, sex, income level, current car — that now becomes available to General Motors in easily accessible electronic form. However, in this as in other advertising models, whether or not to click onto the ad in the first place is up to the user — a notion that is deeply troubling to executives in older advertising-dependent media. "A lot of people are bothered by advertising online in its current state," wrote Barbara Love of Cowles Business Media in November 1994. "The next generation of online services are expected to address ways to make the user want to select advertising."[9]

The question is not whether the information highway will be a vehicle for commerce — it will be, both as an advertising medium and as a vehicle for direct sales. And to a certain extent, it should be. But there is still room to decide whether there will also be substantial space for noncommercial use and public access, which in the development of radio and television happened only imperfectly in Canada and hardly at all in the United States.

To a certain extent, this outcome was a function of the scarcity of available channels and the high cost of producing and distributing radio and especially television programs. Noncommercial space in Canada took the form of taxpayer-supported federal and provincial networks — the CBC, TVOntario, Radio-Québec and the like. The United States developed a somewhat different brand of noncommercial television, the Public Broadcasting System, financed by viewers and corporate donors as well as government grants. All of these networks provide forms of programming that are generally not available on commercial networks and serve as outlets for some producers of content who might be shut out if all of television, instead of only most of it, were governed by commercial criteria. What they do not do, however, is provide broad public access to television production and distribution.

The need for such access was supposed to be filled by the community-access channel each cable company is required to supply. But with its low budget and homey feel, what British Columbia writer Kim Goldberg has called the "barefoot channel" has been consigned to an even more distant margin of the overall television picture than noncommercial networks. Whether it is because cable companies have provided the community-access channel grudgingly or because community groups have not used it creatively, most of what appears on these channels is not very good television. It is no doubt a good thing that an opportunity for television exposure exists for town council meetings, local volleyball tournaments and fledgling rock bands, but this is hardly enough to make a serious dent in the top-down, passive, consumer model that has dominated television since the beginning. It is no accident that Rogers sent Bruce Matheson of its community channel department to present the company's point of view to a May 1995 conference on public access to the information highway in Ottawa. To the cable companies, community access equals public relations.

And yet, one of the most compelling promises of the information highway — and its existing prototype, the World Wide Web — lies precisely in the notion of the barefoot channel. For on the inforoute, instead of one barefoot channel hidden among thirty or forty commercial and noncommercial networks, there are potentially as many barefoot channels as there are people who want to use them: anyone with a middling computer system and modest skills in operating it can put up a Web site containing whatever she or he wants to communicate to the world. Time Warner has its Web site, but so does a student in Minnesota who has given the world access to his high school science papers or a couple in Montreal who have posted pictures of their newborn baby.

Nor is this kind of access inherently limited to text and still pictures. The increasing ease and declining expense of video recording and editing are bringing high-quality film production within the range of a much larger number of people. Once bandwidth on the inforoute grows to the point where it can accommodate efficient video transmission, the same could happen for film distribution. Senior CBC producer Mark Starowicz has described this combination of developments as "the Gutenberg Revolution of television, which I define as the moment at which the means of production becomes democratically accessible."[10]

This is the promise; is there anything to stop it from becoming the reality? Perhaps the most obvious danger is the possibility that whoever ends up gaining control of the infrastructure of the information highway — telcos, cablecos or some combination of the two — will also gain control of the content and operate the information highway as an information railway. This, after all, is the way media have always been run in the past. Without some separation of infrastructure from content provision and without the insistence that the owners of information highway infrastructure operate as common carriers, an information highway monopoly could decide that barefoot channels are not worth its time and allocate Web sites (or whatever Web sites become in the future) only to large commercial content providers. There is also the more insidious, and therefore perhaps more plausible, danger of marginalization: the likelihood that no matter how many barefoot channels there are, they will be swamped by the proliferation of commercial content on the inforoute.

The future of electronic media has often been compared to the present state of the magazine industry, primarily in regard to the fragmentation of what was once a relatively unified audience into a mosaic of taste constituencies. The magazine analogy is worth paying attention to from another point of view as well. In Canada, the number of magazines being published has increased dramatically in the last two decades. Technology has been a major factor: the offset press, computer typesetting and desktop publishing have brought production costs down and made it possible for many more people to become magazine publishers (and for almost anyone to publish a 'zine, the stripped-down barefoot channel of the magazine world). A.J. Liebling's adage that a free press is guaranteed only to those who own one remains valid, but its terms change somewhat when the press consists of a personal computer along with some software and peripherals. Judicious state intervention, involving both direct subsidies and legislation (now threatened by the recent World Trade Organization ruling) and preventing American magazines from dumping their editorial content into Canada, has also played a role in encouraging new magazines.

Nevertheless, Canada's newsstands, controlled by intermediaries motivated by commercial considerations, remain dominated by American magazines. Noncommercial Canadian magazines are unavailable on most newsstands and shoved to the back of the few that carry them. These magazines are available predominantly through subscription — in other words, they reach their readers through the common carrier Canada Post. Of course, magazines such as *Kick It Over* and *The Old Fart* don't have the slickness, or the circulation, of *Canadian Living* or *Maclean's*, let alone *Redbook* or *Time*. But they exist. We would do well to ensure that their electronic equivalents, multiplied a thousandfold, exist as well.

Copyright and the Internet

— Who cares about copyright violations?!? It's just a newspaper article. I'm glad he posted it. I missed it in the newspaper.
— Spoken like a true *USENETTER!*
                    Exchange from a Usenet newsgroup on the Internet

Copyright has generally been a technical question for most people, to the extent that they think about it at all. It has to do with some legalities in the front of a book that prohibit them from doing various things they would never think of doing anyway: "No part of this book may be reproduced or transmitted in any form or by any means, electronic or mechanical, including photocopying, or by any information storage and retrieval system, without permission in writing from the publisher."

Now wait a minute. "Including photocopying"? Does that mean that if you take this book down to your neighbourhood copy shop and photocopy two pages that struck you as particularly insightful to send to a friend, you are violating someone's rights?

Technically it means precisely that, although the law would be more likely to kick in if you photocopied eighty copies of chapters two, three and four to distribute to the students in your introductory undergraduate communications course. But either way, the photocopier was the first of a series of inventions that have brought copyright law and people's everyday habits closer together.

In a sense, neither the photocopier nor more recent innovations such as computer networks have changed anything with respect to copyright law. Hence the Information Highway Advisory Council's conclusion "that all digital works, including multimedia works, have sufficient protection under existing categories of works in the Copyright Act."[11] A copyright violation is a copyright violation, whether it involves photocopying two pages from this book or printing and selling a pirate edition of *The Celestine Prophecy*. The second, however, is both more difficult to carry out and easier to detect than the first. In other words, the question is one of enforcement.

Although photocopiers have been in widespread use since the 1960s, it was not until the late 1980s that a serious effort was undertaken to compensate Canadian writers, artists and publishers for the circulation of photographically reproduced copies of their works. The Canadian Reprography Collective, known as Cancopy, has been engaged in working out a system to monitor the photocopying of Canadian works, collect a small fee for each copy and distribute the funds to the writers, artists and publishers concerned. The system appears to work reasonably well for books but less so for magazines, where contracts between writers and publishers tend to be more informal and where a single photocopied page can routinely involve the rights of several artists and writers as well as the publisher.

Meanwhile, Cancopy has also expressed interest in administering the even more complex area of electronic rights. If the photocopier made copyright violation easy and enforcement difficult, the computer network raises possibilities that have led many people to argue convincingly that the whole concept of copyright as we have known it may be obsolete.

If you have material in digital form, copying it and sending it to a friend no longer even requires the trip to the neighbourhood copy shop. With a keystroke, the material can be forwarded to your friend's e-mail address — or to an entire mailing list. Or, like the newspaper article mentioned earlier, it can be posted to a newsgroup where any interested Net surfer can read it. Forwarding a whole article, or a book, is inherently no more difficult than forwarding a couple of pages (although newsgroups, which tend to favour the short and snappy, would frown on your posting a book). Even if the material is in the form of ink on paper rather than digital bits, the same options may be open to you. If you have a scanner (available for a few hundred dollars) and the right software in your computer, you can put the material in digital form and then proceed as before.

Electronic communication offers other prospects as well. If you buy a book in a bookstore, say George Gilder's *Life after Television*, you can be reasonably confident that what is between the covers is something Gilder wrote, or at least something he approved. Tampering with a book generally leaves traces that are easily apparent to a reader. Gilder's hymns to technology and the free market also circulate widely on the Internet. If you forward the latest Gilder, you can forward it exactly as it comes to you; alternatively, you can add to it, delete from it, change it. You can be honest and flag the changes you made, but if you don't, the casual reader is unlikely to know the difference.

On one level, copyright problems of this sort are merely side-effects of the qualities that give computer networks their air of excitement in the first place. One of the slogans of cyberspace, after all, is "Information is free." To many people this means not only accessible to the public but also available without providing compensation to the information's creator. And if information can be altered as it travels, some people see that as merely a welcome breakdown of the hierarchical relationship between author and reader.

For creators, however, these developments are a mixed blessing. On the one hand, creators are generally grateful when someone shows enough interest in their product to take the trouble to buy, borrow, copy or download it. Furthermore, creators are often avid consumers of information as well, and with that hat on they tend to believe in "Information is free" with as much fervour as other information consumers. On the other hand, creators are plagued by the nagging sense that life would be better if they could somehow be compensated for their work.

Some commentators have argued that that sense, rooted in the age of ink on paper, is something they need to get over. Esther Dyson suggested in *Wired* in mid-1995:

> While not all content will be free, the new economic dynamic will operate as if it were. In the world of the Net, content (including software) will serve as advertising for services such as support, aggregation, filtering, assembly and integration of content modules, or training of customers in their use. Intellectual property that can be copied easily likely *will* be copied. It will be copied so easily and efficiently that much of it will be distributed free in order to attract attention or create desire for follow-up services that can be charged for.[12]

Dyson is deeply immersed in the computer world, and her model for "content" tends to be computer software, where the kinds of ancillary services she evokes represent a significant complement, and sometimes even an alternative, to actual sale of the product. Software companies such as Microsoft and Lotus periodically inveigh against unauthorized copying of their products — an estimated 60 per cent of the software in use is pirated. And yet, all this piracy has not prevented the reigning monarch of software, Microsoft's Bill Gates, from becoming the world's wealthiest human being.

But there are other kinds of content besides computer software, and here the prospects become murkier. Advertising support is one possibility — this is after all the mechanism through which television programs have been distributed "free" to viewers since the 1940s. But as every television viewer knows, this mechanism has its limitations. Furthermore, for most Canadian television viewers, content is no longer free; it comes at the price of a monthly payment to their local cable company. As television fragments into multiple channels, producers of content rely decreasingly on advertising and increasingly on other mechanisms such as cable subscription fees and pay-per-view.

Dyson has other suggestions as well: "Would you pay more for Michael Crichton's words, or for the ability to suggest a new plot to him or name a hero? How much was his book worth to the movie *Disclosure*? How much was his name worth?" In other words, Michael Crichton can make money just from *being* Michael Crichton. But what about all the writers and other creators who are not Michael Crichton? Dyson has not forgotten them either: "With the means of production growing cheaper and easier because of the Net, a bifurcation will take place: more and more people will produce material for smaller audiences of their friends, while those seeking large audiences will give their stuff away or seek payment from a sponsor — and try to persuade influencers to recommend it."[13] The "bifurcation" she envisions is a likely eventuality, but it undercuts one of the most tantalizing promises of the information highway: the prospect of direct communication between creator and audience, free of the mediating priesthood of editors, publishers, producers and network executives.

To be sure, there are technical fixes that will mitigate some of these problems. In particular, encryption technology makes it possible to deliver content only to people who have bought and paid for it — perhaps in a form in which it cannot be infinitely copied. Such measures may be necessary, but again, they undercut the promise of a radically new relationship between creator and audience.

At the same time, the inforoute does not eliminate the need for creators to be compensated for their work. Nor does it reduce the importance of distributing content that lies somewhere between mass-market entertainment and the electronic equivalent of vanity publishing. It is not only the legal aspects of electronic publishing that remain to be settled. The economics of electronic publishing are still very much an underdeveloped area. Publishers of online magazines — which include major corporations such as Time Warner and Condé Nast — still haven't figured out how to make money from these publications, and continue to regard them primarily as promotion for their ink-and-paper products. Not even Microsoft has figured out how to make money from *Slate* magazine, launched in 1996 as an exclusively online publication. Contemplating the financial performance of his company's World Wide Web site in late 1995, one senior media executive is reported to have said, "I now understand what a black hole looks like." And yet large and small publishers alike continue to regard an online presence as an important part of their business.

One conclusion that may perhaps be drawn from all this is that, in Canada at least, the advent of the information highway makes government support for culture more rather than less important. Even the free market–oriented Information Highway Advisory Council recognized the need for government money to ensure the presence of Canadian content on the inforoute. This is, of course, nothing new. Through the CBC, the federal government compensates Canadian creators for making their works freely available to radio and television audiences. Since 1987, through Public Lending Right, Ottawa has compensated Canadian writers and other creators of books for making their works freely available in libraries. The need for a comparable mechanism to compensate creators for making their works freely available on the information highway, where both legal and economic questions are just beginning to be explored, is even clearer.

Censorship and Privacy

As with copyright regulations, the limitations on free speech implied in laws against defamation, pornography and hate literature apply in theory to electronic communications as much as they do to any other kind of communication. But again, as with copyright regulations, the growth of electronic communications creates problems of enforcement that call the whole theory into question. "Of course," says the Information Highway Advisory Council, "the rule of law applies with equal force to the Information Highway."[14] Yet if matters were really that simple, would it be necessary to state such an obvious fact?

Philosophically, the question of what restrictions on free speech are justifiable in a free society is a morass. When we decide to restrict the free circulation of pornography, we sometimes end up removing Margaret Laurence novels from library shelves; when we decide free speech is sacrosanct, we end up with seductive cigarette ads in magazines. But so long as there are relatively few book, magazine and newspaper publishers and radio and television broadcasters, any restrictions on free speech that we choose to write into legislation can at least be enforced. Enforcement is also enhanced by the circumstance that some of this material needs to be physically transported across borders: Canada's most assiduous censors have been Canada Customs officers.

Electronic communication for public consumption involves a much larger number of producers and completely penetrable borders. As a result, scare stories about the kind of content available on the Internet quickly became a staple of media coverage of the information highway. CBC television's *Prime Time News* ran a documentary in late 1994 on the use of the Internet by neo-Nazi and other far-right groups. Other media items have highlighted pornography, doomsday cults or banned information about the Karla Homolka case. According to the documentary about neo-Nazis, attempts to eliminate content that broke Canadian law were ineffective because the originators could simply route their messages through other countries.

Prominent members of the Internet community such as Jim Carroll have also pointed to the sheer impossibility of monitoring the huge volume of communication on the Internet. In December 1994, an employee of the Canadian Human Rights Commission expressed concern about "the use of the Internet by white-supremacists, Holocaust deniers, gay bashers and other elements of the extreme right" and said he was doing research "to determine what measures could be considered to control the use of the Net for this type of purpose." Carroll replied,

> Congratulations on your study. However, the first thing you should do is understand that the 'Net is essentially uncontrollable. The only way to control content on the 'Net would be to unplug our entire national telephone system. That is the *only way*.

In a similar vein, another participant in the debate, posting from British Columbia, acknowledeged that it would be "technically feasible to monitor the Internet and detect, for example, the transport of smutty pictures and language."

> There would be a need for 115,740 inspectors working concurrently at every minute of every day. Total inspector staff would be roughly 555,555 and at a cost of say, $30,000 per each, we'd use about $16 billion yearly. We might be able to cut that in

half by automating the search for nasty words. Nasty pics would probably still need to be viewed by each member of a panel.

In moving towards passage of a bill banning indecent speech on the Internet, the U.S. Congress was not deterred by such obstacles — or by an Internet Day of Protest in which more than 20,000 people expressed their displeasure through phone calls, faxes and e-mail to Congressional offices. How effective such legislation will be now that it is in place remains to be seen. According to Jim Carroll, the best control on abusive content is the vigilance of the Internet community, which can police itself through such mechanisms as flaming participants who violate its codes.

Another and perhaps more promising approach has become associated with the name of another British Columbian, Ken McVay. After coming across some antisemitic material on the Internet, McVay began reading widely on the Holocaust, transcribing relevant information into his computer and posting it to refute the material he had seen. As his files grew, an increasing number of requests for information poured into his e-mail box, and he was soon devoting all his time to Holocaust research and documentation. Now aided by some 150 volunteers and in the process of constructing what may be the world's largest Holocaust-resource World Wide Web site, he lectures to Jewish groups and has been awarded the Order of British Columbia.

The question of controls on content is not limited to areas where the content is clearly offensive. Ursula Franklin, peace activist and retired University of Toronto metallurgy professor, notes that, like the ocean, cyberspace is being used as "a global dump." People dump their garbage into the ocean; people dump their useless information into the Internet. Like the ocean, the Internet belongs to everybody and it belongs to nobody. Junk can eliminate good material by driving it out or by simply burying it, Franklin says. We don't have the mechanisms yet to pull out the good stuff efficiently.

While denying that he is advocating censorship, former Quebec cabinet minister Claude Forget, a member of the Information Highway Advisory Council and coauthor of the 1995 book *The Medium and the Muse,* sees the need for "intermediaries" of the type found, for example, in the provision of financial services or the distribution of physical goods. On the Internet, users have to sift through mountains of information, making the system inefficient. They don't have choices made for them the way cable TV subscribers do, for instance, and this freedom gets in the way of efficiency. Forget argues that Internet users need not only a road map but also a "travel guide" to help them choose where to go, and the existence of consultants or intermediaries would achieve great savings in time.

Internet road maps have taken the form of search engines, often with whimsical names like Archie (a search tool for the file transfer protocol or FTP utility, which allows users to download files from faraway computers) or Yahoo! (one of the most popular search tools for the World Wide Web). Thus, an Archie search will give someone who wants to use FTP to research a particular topic the addresses of computers that have information on that topic. Similarly, Yahoo! will direct a user who types in a word or words to a list of Web sites that have information matching those words. Started by two Stanford University graduate students, Yahoo! attracted the attention of venture capitalists who were impressed with its potential as a medium for targeting advertising at specific interest groups. Yahoo!'s shares are now publicly traded, as are the shares of other search engine companies such as Lycos and Excite. In Canada, the growing market for Web navigation instruments fuelled the growth of a Waterloo, Ontario–based firm called Open Text Corporation which, in its early stages, worked with Yahoo! as a "strategic partner."

"The information that matters the most in electronic environments is not information," comments Paul Saffo of the Institute for the Future, an organization that studies the effects of technology on society. "It's meta-information. It's information about information." Typically, search tools have not told users anything about the nature or quality of the available information; to find that out, they need to connect to the actual site. Newer versions, now known as "media navigation services," begin to approximate Forget's travel guide model. Excite, for example, offers an option called "Net Reviews," a critical survey of sites in a variety of subject areas.

But while the growth of services of this sort can be seen as a necessary move to bring the chaos of the Internet under some control, it is precisely the Net's unmediated nature that has constituted a large part of its appeal and given rise to much of the writing about its democratic potential. Forget's distinction between censors and "intermediaries" is reminiscent of an explanation of the difference between Soviet and North American television offered to one of the authors by a Soviet journalist during the Brezhnev era. "We call them censors," the journalist said. "You call them producers." It is both the blessing and the curse of the Internet that it is not entirely in the control of producers, or at least not yet.

Perhaps the only other Internet-related issues that arouse as much public passion as offensive content and censorship are questions of privacy and security. These have always been issues in relation to electronic communication — indeed, in relation to any form of communication. Anyone who gives a credit card number over the telephone is taking a risk, but it is a risk that most people accept. Anyone who keys a credit card number into a computer network is also taking a risk, and this is one that most people have been much slower to accept. Hence, "electronic shopping malls" often end up with an 800 number for people to call to order the product on offer.

Fear of using one's credit card online is perhaps a crystallization of a diffuse nervousness and unease directed towards computer networks (the flip side of the enthusiasm and hype that also surrounds them) and especially towards what those computer networks might know about *you*. Computer networks of all kinds make available information about the user in a form that is easily accessible and can be easily tabulated (and perhaps easily cracked). Using a debit card at the grocery store gives retailers and manufacturers detailed information about your shopping habits, down to whether you buy Coke or Pepsi.

For the inforoute to realize its potential as a medium of commerce, squeamishness about using credit and debit cards will somehow have to be overcome. At the time of writing, an intense race was on to develop a method of transporting credit card information over the Internet that people would regard as secure, pitting a Visa-Microsoft partnership in one corner against a MasterCard-Netscape team in the other. But not everybody wants to use credit cards, and so a viable form of anonymous electronic cash, which could be used to pay for goods through computer networks, will be equally important. A race to introduce an exchange medium of this kind is also underway. Electronic cash could be analogous to the cards used in library photocopy machines; the user would insert such a card in a computer to effect an electronic transfer of funds.

Another aspect of protecting electronic communication is encryption. Sophisticated means of encryption have been developed. One that has attracted particular attention is public-key encryption (one version of which is known as "Pretty Good Privacy" (PGP), which provides a secure electronic "signature" verifying that a message actually comes from the person purporting to send it. Such a system could have prevented the embarrassing hoax perpetrated on Ontario's then-premier, Bob Rae, in late 1994 when a false message allegedly coming from his office was widely circulated. Ontario Conservative leader Mike Harris vigorously denounced Rae for this security lapse. After Harris became premier in 1995, a similar hoax was perpetrated on him, and he cancelled his office's Internet account.

While public-key encryption has gained wide support among Internet users, another form of encryption called the Clipper chip, proposed in the United States in 1994, ran into fierce opposition because the federal government would have had the power to decode all messages — a power it claimed it needed to catch criminals using computer communication. Computer security raises the same questions that have long troubled us regarding security in the nonelectronic world. Are the people who are claiming to protect us any more trustworthy than those they are claiming to protect us from? Given that all social interaction, electronic or otherwise, depends on a willingness to take reasonable risks, might we become so concerned about security that we lose the benefits the interaction was supposed to provide in the first place?

Computer networks also raise questions about the very nature of privacy. Some forms of computer communication, such as electronic mail, clearly are, and should be, private (although questions about electronic mail security have certainly been raised). Other forms, such as Web sites and articles posted to discussion forums of various sorts, are clearly public. But the flexibility of computer communications and the ease with which messages can be distributed and forwarded to lists of the sender's choosing create numerous grey areas, and the boundaries between private and public are still being defined.

Gender and Identity

Another boundary that has become blurred on computer networks is the line between the masculine and the feminine. These networks are coming into widespread use at a time when gender roles are becoming increasingly fluid, in North American society at least. The growing presence of women in traditionally masculine domains such as politics and the professions is the clearest manifestation of this tendency. Traditionally feminine activities such as child care and housework have been slower to gain acceptance as appropriate pursuits for men, but there has been some movement in that direction as well. Over time, these developments, among the most significant social changes of the late twentieth century, have raised questions about the very meaning of masculinity and femininity.

Other elements of identity have been subject to the same pressures. "We are becoming fluid and many-sided," writes psychologist Robert Jay Lifton. "Without quite realizing it, we have been evolving a sense of self appropriate to the restlessness and flux of our time. This mode of being differs radically from that of the past, and enables us to engage in continuous exploration and personal experiment."[15] Until very recently, gender has been perhaps the element of identity most resistant to the fragmenting forces of modernity. While the rigid social strata of feudalism are a distant historical memory in most western societies, people still have personal experience of the idea of separate spheres for women and men, and conventions of language and dress reflect this idea to some degree even now. In the long run, however, gender is no more immune to change than any other social barrier or form of identity.

Computer networks allow a person to interact with others in a context where nothing is known about them except their online persona. Many Internet participants value this feature of their chosen medium. Thus, Thomas W. Cook posted to the can.infohighway newsgroup from Queen's University in Kingston in January 1995:

> The Internet is the great equalizer. Readers of my messages don't know if I'm an "angst-ridden teenager," an "unemployed writer" or a "university professor." I could be male or female and my skin could be any colour of the rainbow. If someone is going to judge me, they have to do it based on my words and my ideas.

Or as a 1993 P. Steiner cartoon in the *New Yorker* said it, "On the Internet, no one knows you're a dog."[16] In this climate, it is not surprising that a person of one sex will sometimes take on a persona of the other sex — particularly males taking on female personae. This has happened in Internet newsgroups, but especially in the role-playing games known as MUDs (Multi-User Dungeons).

"MUDs are an identity workshop," writes Amy Bruckman of the Massachusetts Institute of Technology, who has studied the phenomenon. Bruckman describes a MUD as "a text-based multi-user virtual-reality environment." Participants create characters who build a social milieu by communicating with other characters within a defined space. A character can be male, female, gender-neutral or plural, irrespective of the sex and number of the creator(s). "Without makeup, special clothing, or risk of social stigma," writes Bruckman, "gender becomes malleable in MUDs."[17] Some MUDs, notably the variety known as MOOs (MUDs, Object-Oriented), offer a broad range of gender options, including such possibilities as spivak and splat. "Because the pronouns assigned to the participant efface gender distinctions," notes Shannon McRae, a doctoral candidate at the University of Washington, "a spivak can have any morphological form and genital structure e devises for emself."[18]

Technological changes and changes in gender relations have often been closely related. Thus, the introduction of the typewriter towards the end of the nineteenth century helped create the conditions in which the male clerk was replaced by the female typist and stenographer as part of a reorganization of office work. A century later, it has become commonplace to ascribe the latest sex/gender developments to computer networks. Thus, a *Newsweek* cover story on bisexuality in July 1995 called the Internet the "most significant" of the factors creating a "bisexual moment": "The Internet has emerged as a safe harbor where users can play fluidly with gender, both their own and that of their virtual partners."[19] Similarly, Washington lawyer Martine Rothblatt, author of *The Apartheid of Sex*, sees the future capacity of the information highway to transmit virtual reality images as an important element in bringing about her projected utopia in which the very category of gender as we know it today is abolished:

> When cyberspace is enhanced by virtual reality, there are innumerable opportunities to "try on" genders as part of cybersexual explorations. First there is creating your image. A digital camera in front of your PC will put your image on the screen. From there you take charge as the editor. Feminize the face, masculinize the voice, "morf" the body, androgynize the clothes — all will be readily possible using virtual reality clip art and drawing tools.[20]

The same skepticism needs to be applied to predictions of this sort as to other utopian claims about the Internet. The widespread questioning of received notions of gender is a long-term change in society that probably would have taken place with or without computer networks. But computer networks clearly do have the capacity to contribute further to a blurring of traditional gender roles, and indeed to a breakdown of divisions among social roles in general.

It is all the more ironic, then, that at least in its early stages the information highway has been largely a male bastion. For as it exists today in the form of computer networks, the information highway is essentially a product of the computer culture of the 1980s. And this is a culture made up primarily of people who are comfortable with technology and uncomfortable with authority, at least in its traditional forms. These people are predominantly male. In the mid-1990s, estimates of the proportion of male users on various computer networks ranged from 65 to 90 per cent. A 1995 Georgia Tech survey found that the typical World Wide Web user is a thirty-year-old educated male who works with computers.

Some male commentators, including George Gilder, have ascribed the imbalance to biological factors. Computer consultant Karen Coyle disagrees:

What we will need is a conspiracy of sisters that begins with the recognition that there is nothing inherently masculine about computers. We must learn to read the computer culture for the social myth that it is. And we have to teach our younger generation of women that they are free to explore computers in their own way and to draw their own conclusions about the usefulness of these machines.[21]

A March 1997 Nielsen survey reported that women constituted 42 per cent of online users. As access to computer networks becomes more of a mass phenomenon, the previously untapped female market is being reached. Recent marketing trends reflect a strong effort to reposition the computer as a "family" device. Thus, the cover of *Newsweek*'s summer 1995 special issue, "Computers and the Family," shows former football star Joe Montana, his wife Jennifer and their four children in an outdoor setting. Five-year-old Nathaniel Montana is excitedly engaged with his laptop computer. Similarly, Microsoft ads for its Microsoft Bob interface (which McGill University doctoral candidate Leslie Regan Shade describes as "the Forrest Gumpization of computer interfaces") show a white nuclear 1950s-style family grouped around the computer.

Other technologies have undergone a similar evolution. Telephones were initially promoted as a business device. "Seeing their technology as a business-to-business service," writes Ellen Lupton of the Cooper-Hewitt Museum in New York, "phone executives dismissed women's talk as 'idle chatter' that tied up the lines." It was not until the late 1920s that AT&T marketers began actively to encourage women to socialize on the phone.[22]

The development of easier-to-use interfaces is helping free computer network use from its "techie" origins. But if Karen Coyle is right, and we believe she is, sex disparity is more a question of the culture of the Internet than of its technical complexity, which is in principle no more alien to women than to men. With little external regulation, the Internet has enforced its own code of behaviour, primarily through its characteristic form of verbal abuse known as flaming. This "Wild West" culture has been seen as especially intimidating to women. The analogy can be pursued: the white population of the early West was, after all, overwhelmingly male. But as the early, pioneering, vigilante-justice era fades, so does the sex disparity. The female-to-male ratio of the population of contemporary Nevada or Colorado is not much different from the American average.

AlphaCom, the much more polite computer network that links Ontario literacy providers, a predominantly female group, is widely used and highly valued, although it is more difficult to use than some of the newer Internet interfaces and commercial services such as CompuServe or America Online. And it could be supposed that as a generation that has grown up with computers in their homes and schools reaches adulthood, the female as well as the male members of that generation will use computer networks.

Community and the Internet

Closely related to identity is community; the questions "Who am I?" and "Who are we?" cannot be completely separated from each other. The effect of the Internet and the information highway on community has been the subject of a vigorous debate. For some observers, computer networks are helping to create new forms of community. Thus, political theorist Mark Poster suggests that "there are surely new modes of association in the bulletin boards and MOOs and MUDs. ... When human beings, with or without the significant mediation of machines, interact and exchange symbols, there is community of some sort. The problem is not whether MOOs and bulletin boards are communities, but how they are communities."[23]

Howard Rheingold, who became involved in the online world through a San Francisco–based bulletin board called the WELL, entitled his book on computer-mediated communication *The Virtual*

Community. He describes how the WELL helped one of its members deal with the crisis brought on by his son's leukemia. "The model of the WELL and other social clusters in cyberspace as 'places,'" Rheingold writes, "is one that naturally emerges whenever people who use this medium discuss the nature of the medium."[24] Rheingold is careful not to press the claims of the virtual community too far, but the sense of community that he feels binds him to other WELLites emerges clearly from the pages of his book.

Others, however, see computer networks as contributing to the breakdown of what remains of our traditional communities. Thus, John Gray wrote in the Manchester *Guardian* in April 1995:

> Real communities are always local — places in which people have put down roots and are willing to put up with the burdens of living together. The fantasy of virtual community is that we can enjoy the benefits of community without its burdens, without the daily effort to keep delicate human connections intact. Real communities can bear these burdens because they are embedded in particular places and evoke enduring loyalties. In cyberspace, however, there is nowhere that a sense of place can grow, and no way in which the solidarities that sustain human beings through difficult times can be forged. We should reject the offer of the Internet communities to deliver us from the unchosen constraints of local life.[25]

The historian of telecommunications in Canada, Robert E. Babe, is a more strident proponent of this view:

> The Information Highway will emphasize communication designated for audiences defined on bases other than geography: for example income, class, occupation, hobbies, sex, age, race, tastes, type of accommodation, specialized knowledge and so forth.... By contrast, nation states, communities and legislative processes are all defined on the basis of geography. The "Information Highway", therefore, by expanding transmission capacity to the home, will help break down local or indigenous communication, substituting in its place a "cyber-community" or "virtual-community" — with definite political economy implications.... The world becomes the stage in which individuals and those organizations delimited geographically (for instance national governments) become rendered quite powerless.

Babe concludes that "all those with a love of life, democracy and of community should now be pushing to stop the Information Highway before it begins."[26]

So who is right? Clearly, computer networks make it possible for us to communicate with some people more closely, frequently and immediately. They also make it less necessary, and perhaps more difficult, to relate to the local communities in which we live. On balance, is this a gain or a loss? Do computer networks represent a rebirth of community, or the last nail in its coffin?

We will not attempt anything so ambitious as a definition of community, which belongs to the realm of philosophers and social theorists. Certainly, what the word *community* conjures up for most of us is local and compact: a small town, or perhaps an urban neighbourhood, with people who mostly know one another and participate in common economic, social, cultural, civic and religious institutions. There is much that is admirable in this picture. But the conclusion that all communities necessarily have to be geographically based does not automatically follow.

For large numbers of people in the western world, including most of those who are likely to be communicating through computers, the compact local community within which most of one's significant human interactions take place belongs to the past. Your aged parents in Winnipeg, your daughter in Somalia, your college buddy on assignment in Beijing, your scientific colleague in Germany and your lifelong friend who is working in California may be more important presences in your life than your neighbours in Burnaby or Laval. Furthermore, "real" communities have always had their narrow side, and belonging to a racial, religious or sexual minority, for example, can make you feel very lonely within them. If computer networks can help people communicate and maintain elements of community across geographical boundaries, or find soulmates who are geographically distant from them but close in other ways, then these networks are performing a valuable service.

On the other hand, Babe has identified a very real difficulty. All our political structures are geographically based. If we enhance communities that cross geographical boundaries at the expense of local ones, the effect will be to weaken national political structures. The beneficiaries will be those institutions that are effectively organized across geographical lines — in other words, multinational corporations. This is why Babe urges Jean Chrétien's government to "reverse policies embraced by the Mulroney Tories that lead to death. There is no better place to begin than by scrapping the Information Highway."[27]

Babe's plea draws us into the fascinating debate over whether political units form the most sensible boundaries for the flow of information, any more than they do for flows of material goods and people. This, in turn, brings to mind the dreaded G-word, globalization, whose relationship to the information highway we will explore further in Chapter 6. Babe's argument fits into a school of writing on globalization which implies that almost everything valuable and distinctive in national identities risks getting wiped out as huge multinational corporations, including entertainment giants, leave a worldwide mark.

We are far more sympathetic to the notion that both global information exchange and global free trade offer great potential advantages to broad sectors of humanity. However, to achieve these advantages, the elimination of trade barriers would have to be balanced by an internationalism that was driven by labour, environmental and social groups working at the local or national level to oppose unfettered corporate power, and these groups would have to reach across international boundaries and join forces to exert their influence at the increasingly important global level.[28] The inforoute is among the forces that are making such international ties necessary, indeed urgent, and it could also be among the instruments for creating these ties.

Babe is correct in arguing that governments still have essential roles to play, neoliberal views to the contrary notwithstanding. Governments, in many places the democratic embodiment of the people they represent, must band together to restrain and diminish the depredations that form an unfortunate backdrop to the undoubted advantages offered by transnational trade and information flows. Broad conflicts that pit corporate elites against workers and their families at the national level often occur in even starker form at the global level, and it is not by hiding behind nationalist or protectionist banners that those at the middle or bottom of the heap are going to resolve such disputes in their own favour. Policies and attitudes that aim to create justice and equity within the boundaries of a nation-state need equally to be applied outside these boundaries.

Nor is it helpful to try to opt out of the global flow of information. Canadians already have access to such manifestations of the information highway as the World Wide Web and satellite television. The Canadian government may be able to speed up or delay some elements of the highway, broaden or limit access to it and influence its content — and it is important for the government to act intelligently in doing all of those things. But it is no more practicable (or desirable) for the government to "scrap" the information highway than to scrap the telephone.

While we are generally optimistic about the effects of the inforoute on community, we do not of course mean to deny the special value of face-to-face contact, even for those who are most marginalized in their geographical communities. "I do wonder about leaning too heavily on the Usenet," wrote one contributor to a sexual-minority newsgroup. "I think that it is a mistake to look to us for the kind of support that is best obtained from 'real' not cyber folk." Another writer agreed: "In the long run, YES, support from real people is essential, at least for those of us who live in the real world.... The support I received [online] was an important part of my journey. But as I gained support in the real world, my need for electronic support declined."

In the modern world, face-to-face contact has long been supplemented by other tools for communicating and maintaining community, such as the telephone and the postal service. Computer networks are simply another instrument in this toolbox, whatever their real advantages (speed, many-to-many communication, ready-made supportive networks) or novelty value. But none of the tools of communication are equally accessible to everyone. While the great majority of North Americans can afford telephones, a significant number cannot, and on a world scale, a telephone is a luxury good. This is even more true of the necessary elements of participation in computer networks: a computer, a modem and a subscription to an online service of some kind. Is differential access to computer networks creating what U.S. Representative Ed Markey (D — Massachusetts) calls "information apartheid"? Suneel Ratan wrote in a special issue of *Time* in the spring of 1995,

> All of today's information roads charge tolls, sometimes hefty ones, that effectively bar even many of those who manage to put together the price of a secondhand computer. The situation is further complicated by the tendency of telecommunications companies to place the new information networks in more affluent communities, bypassing, at least for the moment, poorer rural and inner-city areas.[29]

Canada's Information Highway Advisory Council acknowledged these concerns and identified "universal, affordable and equitable access" as a goal of a "national access strategy." The council then engaged in its usual genuflection to the free market, even while acknowledging that it might not be a perfect instrument for meeting this goal and that some government intervention might be required: "In a genuinely competitive environment, the market determines prices, and services pay for themselves. However, market forces occasionally fail to provide universal access at affordable prices."[30] Meanwhile, the "free market," in the form of the monopoly or near-monopoly power of the telephone companies, has been acting in ways that could seriously restrict access to the inforoute.

Bell Canada's proposal to establish a metering system for local calls (which would apply only to business accounts, initially at least, and which the company scrapped in early 1997 in favour of higher fixed rates) put online activists on alert. Steve Withers posted from New Zealand in April 1995:

> Here in NZ, Telecom brought in local call charging for busi-nesses. Their profits went up by about 50% in one year. They now make NZ$700 million on only 1.8 million phone connec-tions — the bulk of that is business services. Imagine Bell Canada making C$3.5–5 billion/annum....
>
> They want to make more money from the infrastructure they now have while cutting back on money for expansion.
>
> WHAT DOES THIS MEAN TO YOU?
>
> It means you and your kids won't be a part of the information revolution — unless you have a good income. If you are a $30,000 mortgage-belt battler, are you going to let *YOUR* kids sit around on a SLIP connection for hours? No way.

But this angry reaction was only a brief flurry compared to the storm unleashed when Bell imposed a steep rate increase on Internet service providers (ISPs) in November 1995. Bell maintained that it had been charging the ISPs the wrong rate all along, and made the change as soon as it discovered the error. The Centrex tariff Bell had been charging, it turned out, didn't apply to lines hooked up to computers, which were considered Information System Access Lines and were by that token subject to a much higher tariff. The fact that the ISPs had contracts with Bell specifying the Centrex tariff (which, at least according to one interpretation, Bell was entitled to break once it discovered it was really supposed to be charging a higher rate) didn't make the increases any more palatable. And suspicions of Bell's motives were raised by the circumstance that its parent company was about to launch its own Internet service through its WorldLinx subsidiary. ISPs and Internet users reacted. One of the milder posts came from Jacques Gélinas:

> Situation ante: Tiny ISPs offer extra cheap rates ($10/month) and attract many customers. WorldLinx cannot compete at these prices (advertising alone costs too much).
>
> Situation now: Half of the tiny ISPs will go belly up, freeing many customers and making room at the upper end for WorldLinx.
>
> Business is business, and the fittest subsidiaries of monopolistic giants survive.

Communications consultant Ian Angus argued against interpreting Bell's action as a conspiracy to drive out the ISPs and leave a large share of the market open for WorldLinx. He suggested instead that "this case is a stunning confirmation of Angus's Law, which states: 'Do not attribute to conspiracy that which can reasonably be explained by incompetence.'" But either way, it was also a stunning demonstration of what happens when questions of access to the information highway are left to the "free market."

The Value of Accessibility

In June 1995, on the occasion of the annual Hebrew Book Week, the editors of the Israeli daily *Ma'ariv* expressed the fear that in the computer age the printed book would soon be a thing of the past. While "a title ordered by computer will never supply the sensual pleasure of feeling a book, inhaling its scent, and turning its pages," they wrote, "what is easier, quicker, and more practical will, in the end, overcome that which is merely enjoyable."

Of course, such sentiments could also have been expressed in the face of the revolution brought about by the printing press five hundred years ago. And while looking at an illuminated medieval manuscript still gives us pleasure that a Stephen King paperback will never provide, most people nowadays would agree that the advent of the printing press was, on the whole, a step forward.

But the *Ma'ariv* editors' complaint should not be dismissed out of hand. The advantages of the inforoute are most often expressed in terms of speed, convenience, volume. "When wallet PCs are ubiquitous," writes Bill Gates in a typical passage, "we can eliminate the bottlenecks that now plague airport terminals, theaters, and other locations where people queue to show identification or a ticket."[31]

What about quality, depth, beauty?

These are things the information highway, no matter what form it takes, will not in itself provide. But quality, depth and beauty may become available to people who would previously not have had access to them, and people who create things of quality, depth and beauty may have outlets for them that would not otherwise be there. If the information highway fulfils some of the promises suggested by the Internet, what it will be able to provide is breadth. After all, where did we get the above quote from *Ma'ariv*, a newspaper that is not exactly ubiquitous on Canadian newsstands?

From the Internet.

The Dual Role of the State

One of the more persistent, and in a sense compelling, voices on the political right is that of George Gilder, and one of the more interesting sites on the Internet is where Gilder admirers and Gilder bashers meet. Gilder maintains not only that the unregulated and unencumbered market is the key to building the information highway but also that the great capital pirates such as Mike Milken were the visionary engineers of the system. In an article published in May 1995 in *Forbes ASAP*, entitled "Mike Milken and the Two Trillion Dollar Opportunity," Gilder writes of Milken's grasp of the future information age:

> Focusing on emergent information companies ... Milken channeled a total of some $26 billion into MCI, McCaw, Viacom, TCI, Time Warner, Turner, Cablevision Systems, News Corp. and other cable, telecom, wireless, publishing and entertainment companies. At the time, virtually none of these firms commanded substantial collateral acceptable to a bank, and thus they could have raised these billions nowhere else. Now, these companies are collectively worth some $224 billion and comprise the foundations of a national information infrastructure unrivaled in the world.[1]

After vindicating Milken and suggesting that the savings and loan fiasco would have been avoided if the banks had been able to hold their junk bonds a little longer, Gilder calls for the emergence of a new "visionary." Such a figure is needed to restructure established industrial and commercial enterprises in the United States, liberate their treasuries and free the capital to find and fund the new telecom systems now at the cutting edge of the technological revolution.

Gilder's notion of the vast power and foresight of the unbridled market is confounded both by history and by the actual ongoing relationship between the state and private enterprise in the development of the inforoute. While Gilder's rhetoric may tweak a responsive chord in the heart of every free enterpriser, his is a voice in the wilderness, even in Washington. Commenting on the legislation that emerged from the American Senate in 1995, "Lexington" in *The Economist* noted that the deregulation bill would actually increase regulation in many areas, mainly because the communications industry, which is enormously powerful, would demand it. Every element of that industry — telecoms, cable, broadcasting — wants some other element controlled.

The point man in the American state's efforts to control and regulate the information highway is Vice President Al Gore, whose background makes him a natural for the role. He has long taken an interest in the information highway and as a senator led the debate on special funding for the Internet. His proposals involve more active state involvement, and he appears to want some form of reregulation of communications.

State Involvement or Corporate Control?

In Canada, nationalists have always argued that government regulation is necessary to protect the country's cultural industries from being swamped by foreign influence. Graham Spry's aphorism, "The State or the United States," coined during the debate on public broadcasting in the 1930s, set out the choice in stark terms. Without Ottawa's involvement, Canada would have had a completely Americanized broadcasting system. But on another level, the choice was not so stark as it appeared. There was always the possibility — and indeed the reality — that Canada would have the state *and* the States: we would be part of an international communications system, but this system would have a Canadian component that would owe its existence to state involvement. It is important to keep this pattern in mind as Canada's communications system develops into the information highway.

From its very inception, radio communication in Canada had an international element. Canada's north shore radio service, established at the turn of the century, provided fishermen and navigators with information about weather and ice in treacherous waters. At the same time, it enhanced international communication by reducing by two days the period of communications silence faced by ships crossing the north Atlantic.[2] The Canadian Marconi company was given the franchise and later (1902) federal financial support to develop the north shore radio service.

In the telephone industry, Sir Wilfrid Laurier enabled Bell to operate as a regulated monopoly while setting the precedent for continental rather than national development in 1905, several years after the phone company had come under complete American control. A few years later, Canada created and manufactured a telegraph system that played a large role in the First World War. Also during the First World War, Max Aitken (soon to become Lord Beaverbrook), working as a publicist for the Canadian military, established the War Office Cinematographic Committee, the first-ever instance of state involvement in the production and distribution of motion pictures. He sent nineteen two-person documentary production units to the Western Front to begin coverage in both still and motion-picture formats, and backed up these documentary units with a docudrama unit led by D.W. Griffith, the father of American theatrical film production.

In 1917, the Department of Trade and Commerce established the first Canadian production and distribution unit, which developed into the Canadian Government Motion Picture Bureau in 1923. "These firsts in production and distribution, like many other events in Canadian history," notes media consultant Patrick Crawley, "were not primarily technological innovations but rather were the creation of important new elements of cultural infrastructure. The creation in Canada of different ways to use imported communications technologies and techniques to affect specifically Canadian objectives are the hallmark of this tradition."[3]

By the 1940s the inventor of radar, Robert Watson-Watt, credited the equipment produced by a Canadian crown corporation with being the "radar arsenal of the western world." It can be argued that our main contribution to the Cold War was in the general area of communications (see Chapter 2). This includes installations such as the DEW Line, established on Canadian territory because of our geographical location. The story goes on through the exploits of A.V. Roe, the ill-fated Arrow and the laid-off engineers and technicians who spread out from Brampton, Ontario, to the various NASA locations in the United States. Canada has also participated in the design, manufacture and operation of sophisticated electronic systems and space age paraphernalia, from satellites to the space arm developed by Spar Aerospace. While any number of smaller domestically owned companies were involved, most of the subcontracting was done by branches of American corporations, including Canada's own Northern Telecom (now Nortel), itself a creature of antitrust cases in the United States.

Thus, Canada has participated in the international communications system both as a consumer and as a producer. Our theoreticians and historians have always described communications as the vital nervous system of our vast country even as our communications have become more and more Americanized. And our Americanized communications have fared very well under Canada's regulatory system, despite protestations to the contrary.

Implicit in the history of communications in Canada has been a dual role for the state. It functions as a regulator but it also functions as an organizer-financier. In this latter role, it has promoted and protected private interests. The technological revolution has merely — if "merely" is the right word — created more powerful players with international connections. Most of the debate, and most of the attacks from the right, seem to relate to the state's role as regulator — which is perhaps the less important of its two roles. For the simple fact remains that regulation stems from and is made possible by scarcity: limited capacity for telephone communications, limited bandwidth for radio and television broadcasting. When the scarcity disappears, as in the new universe of unlimited satellite transmissions, regulation becomes difficult or impossible. And yet the relationship between technological advance and deregulation is not always as simple as advocates of the free market suggest.

Its Neanderthal conservatism notwithstanding, the Toronto *Globe and Mail* perhaps had a point when it described the 1994 CRTC hearings as a "fascinating primitive ritual." As far as the *Globe* was concerned, with the unlimited capacity of the new satellites and fibre optic cable, rationing or regulating television signals is both unnecessary and impossible. Technology confounds the bureaucrats and creates the ideal free competitive market:

> If an all-aerobics channel or round-the-clock Geraldo is what the public wants, let its providers take their case where it belongs: before the public.... If six new channels, or 60, want to offer the same thing let them all try.... The consumer ... should decide their fate and soon will.[4]

As appealing and popular as this sounds, there are a number of problems. In the first place, the public does not decide what it will watch on television any more than it decides what it will read in a newspaper. Those decisions are the prerogative of the owners. The essence of the market is not freewheeling and permanent competition. Rather, it is the tendency towards monopoly: as Gilder noted, in an unregulated market the dominant player will very likely drive out the weaker ones. Monopoly is the likely outcome of the scramble in the United States, where the merger and takeover mania of 1994–96 has been reminiscent of the corporate feeding frenzy of the past decade. In this instance Gilder may be prescient.

Corporate control of the media is not new and from time to time the consequences of this control show up with particular clarity. In the United States, for example, ABC publicly apologized for reporting on the manipulation of the nicotine content of cigarettes. This apology was treated as an example of corporate journalism meeting another branch of corporate America and blinking, but it might be more accurate to see it in a somewhat different light. Corporate America is a single entity, and while on many matters there may be competing interests within that entity, in a crunch it exhibits considerable solidarity. The ABC apology was a manifestation of that solidarity. In Canada, as Keith Davey pointed out in one of the long chain of interesting and forgotten studies of media concentration, the issue isn't that publishers fear corporate advertisers. Rather, the issue is that publishers and advertisers are usually part of the same corporate class.

The 1996 takeover of Southam Inc. by Conrad Black's Hollinger Corp. revived concerns about the concentration of ownership in the Canadian newspaper industry. The Southam chain was already the biggest in Canada. Jointly, Southam and Hollinger came to control nearly 50 per cent of daily newspaper circulation, with much of the rest in the hands of chains controlled by Ken Thomson, Pierre Péladeau, Paul Desmarais and Torstar Corp. At times chains have colluded in stamping out competition, as when Southam and what was then FP slaughtered the Montreal *Star*, Ottawa *Journal* and Winnipeg *Tribune* in 1979. More recently the emphasis has been on staff cuts, with many hundreds of jobs vanishing each year — and some of the heaviest slashing occurring at papers newly controlled by Black. Cost-cutting by chains, Southam in particular, even threatened to kill the Canadian Press news agency.

In economic terms, Black at least has shown a commitment to the newspaper industry, unlike the Thomson chain, which has sold or closed a number of its small-town papers and moved instead to a greater emphasis on data services. Some cost-cutting moves at Black-controlled newspapers have provoked outrage, but if there is a silver lining in all this, the cost-cutting may at least contribute to the long-term financial health of the newspaper industry. While Black is a more obvious villain than some of the publishers he has replaced, the differences — apart from the fact that he controls more papers than they did — may turn out not to be all that great. What this episode points to is the weakness of Canadian competition laws, which in turn results from the difficulty of avoiding oligopoly in Canada's tight-knit capitalist community.

Takeover trophies such as the Jerusalem *Post* and *Saturday Night* veered emphatically to the right under Black-appointed editors. But this tendency has not been as noticeable among Canadian daily papers that have fallen under Black's control. Before takeover, these papers tended to reflect the concerns of rich white males, and this has not changed. Readers born before 1960 may recall a CBC radio show called *Capital Report* that included a review of newspaper editorials from across Canada. Nowadays, newspaper editorials are considered too irrelevant and too tiresome to be bothered with in the same way. Readers are more likely to be swayed, of course, by the emphasis given to certain aspects of the news and the selection of stories editors consider worth covering. At the time of writing, the jury is still out on whether Black's pronounced right-wing views are going to make much difference.

Thus, the point the *Globe* really misses is that with all the talk of infinite choice, the communications industry is becoming concentrated in fewer hands and owned by fewer interests. Huge corporations such as Disney and Time Warner control the vast majority of what we see, hear and read, including the news and commentaries. And it is corporate interests that are served — try attacking defence spending in a program sponsored by General Electric or General Motors.

Corporate journalism and corporate control of the cultural, information and entertainment complex have always existed and have always carried the American corporate message both to the natives and abroad. The message gets carried in an increasing variety of media — from clothes, toys, games and sports to books, magazines, computer networks and cable television.

As schools gain access to the inforoute, business is brought directly into the classroom and the corporate cosmology of big business will become central to the curriculum. A similar trend can be seen in a new style of televison coproduction: in one current case, IBM and NBC's business network are working on a historical series about microchip and computer technology, with IBM having the final say on content and presentation.

Moreover, the new media moguls such as Rupert Murdoch and John Malone openly promote their political views over their systems. In a profile of John Malone, journalist Ken Auletta described how Malone can manipulate programs carried over his vast cable networks — to such a degree that his archrival Sumner Redstone of Viacom complained to American regulatory authorities.[5] And Malone is not shy about his gently described "quirky" right-wing views. His hero is Rush Limbaugh, and when Limbaugh's influence was on the rise there was no market in the United States that was closed to him. Even Ontario got Rush every day before many people had heard of him.

In addition to being all over the radio dial in every market, Limbaugh has a forum on CompuServe. Other Republican worthies such as Gov. John Engler of Michigan and former presidential candidate Lamar Alexander have also had online exposure. Also worth noting is National Empowerment Television, a twenty-four-hour conservative cable-television network stitched together by nine groups, including the National Rifle Association and the U.S. Business Industrial Association, along with some bountiful unnamed donors. Republican House Speaker Newt Gingrich is host of one of the network's shows, which reaches an estimated nine million households.

Then there was Rupert Murdoch's $5 million advance to Gingrich for a book to be based on Gingrich's televised (cable again) college history course. Murdoch at the time was fighting for American government approval for him to move aggressively into the American market — partly in partnership with John Malone, who is also a large stockholder in CNN, whose parent Turner Broadcasting became part of Time Warner through the "mother of all media mergers" in August 1995.

A day or so before the announcement of this merger, the *Toronto Star* published an excellent compilation of "cultural cartels" by media reporter Antonia Zerbisias. In her article, Zerbisias described Westinghouse, which recently bought CBS, as the corporation that bribed the late Philippine dictator Ferdinand Marcos with $35 million to allow it to build a nuclear reactor on an active volcano in an earthquake zone. Westinghouse is now Dan Rather's boss.[6]

Zerbisias noted that NBC's *Dateline* has not shown any interest in the Pentagon activities of NBC's owner, General Electric. She suggested that CBS is likely to be similarly reluctant to report on Westinghouse's aggressive campaign to build nuclear reactors in the former Soviet Union should something go awry. The close — indeed integral — relationship between media concerns and defence industry giants such as General Motors, General Electric and now Westinghouse is another aspect of the consolidation and monopolization of the information system. Thinking perhaps of the old Westinghouse of washing machines and refrigerators, many commentators have expressed concern over the lack of (that fashionable word) synergy between CBS and Westinghouse. Westinghouse hasn't made a washing machine or any other appliance for decades. As a major military contractor, however, it has developed some of the most sophisticated spy systems and other electronic wizardry.

The one thing not happening in all the mergers is any democratization of the airwaves or public involvement beyond consumer surveys. If there is an all-aerobics channel in the infinite-channel universe, it will be because Disney wants it.

Tightening corporate control is naturally linked with the demise of public television in both Canada and the United States. The end approaches for the CBC and we merely await the autopsy — will it be suicide, starvation or euthanasia? Moses Znaimer of CITY-TV and MuchMusic now controls what was Alberta public broadcasting and rumours have suggested he will get control of Ontario public television, which the Harris government wants to privatize, for one dollar. And all the while a relentless campaign is waged to speed the end of regulation and redefine out of existence the whole concept of the public interest.

The State as Regulator

In a series entitled "On Ramp" in the *Globe and Mail*, Don Tapscott discussed the putative role of the public sector. The social and economic changes promised by the highway are too profound to be developed by the private sector alone, he suggested. There is a role for government, but that role should not be conceived as in the past:

> Regulated monopolies are characteristic of Canadian communications networks, and Jon Gerrard, Secretary of State for Science, Research and Development, says, "This lack of com-

petition has caused us to fall behind the United States in the provision and price of advanced telecommunications services."[7]

The new role for government is described as one that balances providing public access, assuring service to all areas of the country and creating the proper competitive atmosphere, and provides seed money for specific projects and services.

While technology has advanced enough to frustrate attempts to regulate and allocate channels, where the merger of fibre optics and the computer will lead is not yet clear. A scientific-technological revolution, like any other, is defined as the instant of great change or alteration. As such the term is probably used much too loosely. But a revolution is also a process, in which the beginnings are fairly easily understood but the direction and final result can rarely be anticipated. Just one small illustration will suffice. The technology that creates infinite channels also creates the so-called V-chip, which can control the reception of any program.

Nor is it quite true that the technological imperative makes a mockery out of attempts to control and regulate television and communications in general. To be sure, by undermining the old assumption of bandwidth scarcity and making borders more penetrable, new technologies do change the parameters of regulation and perhaps make it more difficult. Nevertheless, if we look at the area of direct-to-home satellite television, any country with a communications satellite in orbit could rule that domestic receptors and transmitters use it exclusively. This was the burden of the original CRTC ruling giving the Canadian company ExpressVu a direct-to-home satellite broadcast monopoly. This decision was overturned by the Chrétien government for political reasons, not technological ones.

In the same way, technological change does not seem to have stopped the United States from defending its cultural exports and protecting its home market. These interventions are justified in terms of political and economic pressures and threats of a trade war; there is no question of the Americans sitting back and waiting for the abstract and objective march of technology to solve the problem for them. Thus, the split-run magazine issue, which was brought to the fore by technology allowing Time Warner to transmit magazine pages electronically from the United States to be printed in Canada, soon moved out of the technological arena into Parliamentary corridors, lobbyists' offices and ultimately the World Trade Organization.

If we are told in Canada that it is impossible to regulate the march of technology, this idea has never occurred to the Americans. In the United States, the old rules still govern and the state still regulates and intervenes as it sees fit.

The Canadian government may not understand the implications of foreign control of the inforoute — control of the hardware, software and all that flows through the satellites and cables — but the American government certainly does. The United States has always had stringent restrictions on foreign investment in its telecommunications and media sectors. However, in an effort to move into Europe and Asia and to pry open the major world telecommunications markets, in 1995 the United States proposed total free and open access. Speaking to a conference of European business leaders, Vice President Gore declared the Americans' intention to open foreign investment in telecommunications services to all countries that have opened their own markets. It will be interesting to see how long Canada's restrictions on foreign ownership in our telecommunications and media last.

Regulation, Communications and the Market

The relationship of the market to the development of the technology of communication and transportation has a long and complex history, involving the state directly at an early stage. The essential problem is what could be called Ross's Paradox, after the late business journalist Alexander Ross, who posed it in these terms: "I really like small business. And I really don't like big business. But if small business is successful, it grows and becomes big business." The free workings of the market lead to a smaller number of even larger players, eventually creating monopolies. An unrestrained monopoly in transportation and communication affects all other areas of the economy — and stifles the market.

In his book *Telecommunications in Canada*, Robert E. Babe discusses how the telegraph came to Canada. There are many analogies to be made between the pioneering period and the present. We can see how the telegraph system meshed with the technology and the industry of the times, particularly the railways, and how its development was accelerated by the needs of the military as the enforcers of the newly emerging Canadian state.

In the 1930s, Saskatchewan Premier James T. Anderson declared that "two of the most important milestones in the history of the west were the coming of the Mounted Police and the building of the Government Telegraph line" — a synergistic confluence if ever there was one, illustrating well Harold Innis's astute observation concerning the conjuncture of empire with control over communication.[8] The telegraph speeded instructions from the east, while the Mounties ensured compliance in the west.

It is obvious that the movement of information, which is the essence of the highway, was never considered in and of itself. It was rather an efficient means to conduct every other business and enterprise in which society engages. It is thus somewhat misleading to consider the "information highway" to be one specific thing. Moreover, the various media — telephone, cable, wireless and wired transmissions — are variations of the same technology. Babe discusses musical concerts being sent over the telephone lines from city to city in Ontario before the first wireless transmission, which was sent by a Canadian, Reginald Fessenden.

The Canadian state, like every other, moved rapidly into the field of telecommunications. In Canada, part of the motivation was to ensure that the west remained Canadian, and part of the reason for the speed with which the state involved itself, from the most primitive telegraph to the most sophisticated satellites, was the realization that only the most modern and complete communications systems could guarantee the existence of the Canadian state with its massive distances between pockets of population.

The state in Canada has always been forced to interpose itself between potential or actual monopoly and the larger economic interests of the country. It has used several methods. One is nationalization, employed reluctantly when there is absolutely no alternative, and also temporarily. As soon as an alternative appears, "privatization" becomes the issue: Air Canada come most easily to mind. When the market no longer regards state intervention as necessary, it is unceremoniously halted. Think of the late National Energy Program, which was destroyed in Canada by Canadians, albeit with the active encouragement of American interests.

A more favoured method is a regulatory system, such as the CRTC, which protects those interests dependent on the communication and transportation system from the predatory actions of a monopoly while giving the appearance of being a public "watchdog" — and sometimes acting the role. This approach has been especially attractive in Canada, where a relatively weak and vulnerable domestic corporate sector has been spared competition and been able to have its investments and profits secured — thus ironically making it more attractive to foreign investors.

A case in point is the Bell system, which began life in Canada as a franchise Alexander Graham Bell gave his father and exists today in Canada as a sideshow to the pieces of the broken-up American monopoly (an antitrust battle whose outcome many people seem now to regret). Bell is a paradigm of how to use the regulatory system to corporate advantage, while the public interest has remained mainly the stuff of rhetorical documents and earnest departmental communications.

As a country with "too much geography and too little history," as Mackenzie King once said, Canada has moved quickly to embrace and develop every promising new form of transportation and communication and has used every tool possible towards this end. This process has occurred against the backdrop of the nationalist-versus-continentalist, state-versus-free-enterprise, monopoly-versus-competition arguments that have been the hallmark of Canada's development as a capitalist state. Peter Newman has taken this a step further, expressing the notion that Canada's capitalism has been a capitalism with a human face. As is often the case with Newman, the cliché triumphs over content, but he has a point when he writes:

> Canada's mixed economy was a blend uniquely suited to Canada, as the country's forbidding geography and absence of large-scale economies had, for instance, prompted governments to create 464 state enterprises with assets worth $84 billion, in charge of everything from the national airline to the national broadcaster.[9]

We should include our regulatory systems in this general context of what is "uniquely suited to Canada." Along with the pressure to destroy the state enterprises built over the years comes the process of weakening and diluting the mandate of Canada's regulatory agencies, especially in the vital area of communications. Unfortunately, regulatory agencies such as the CRTC sometimes seem intent on making this task easier by repeatedly issuing decisions of the sort that bring the whole process into discredit and by habitually showing excessive indulgence towards the mercenary interests of private broadcasters and cable operators. Some of the companies regulated by the CRTC argue in public that the regulatory system should be merely a mechanism to create a level playing field for various corporate interests, while at the same time using the CRTC as a platform to secure special privileges for themselves. Cynics argue that the CRTC is regulated by these various corporate interests rather than the other way around. Clearly some sort of public oversight is required to make sure that development of the inforoute serves the broad interests of Canada as a whole as well as local and regional interests. The private sector will not do this on its own. It is equally clear that the CRTC is not up to the task.

Regulated Monopolies

In his classic *Principles of Political Economy*, John Stuart Mill wrote:

> When a business of real public importance can only be carried on in an advantageous way upon so large a scale as to render the liberty of competition almost illusory, it is an unthrifty dispensation of the public resources that several costly arrangements should be kept up for the purpose of rendering the community this one service. It is much better to treat it at once as a public function, and if it be not such as government itself, it should be made over entire to the company or association which will perform it on the best terms to the public.

In the context of the various authorities, agencies and commissions that the federal government and some provinces have created since the invention of the telegraph to regulate and control the development of transport and communications in Canada, Mill's mid-nineteenth-century dictum still has some resonance. Over time, Canada has created, protected and coddled a long series of monopolies, both publicly and privately owned.

Some argue that a state-owned monopoly is more likely to ensure lower rates and costs, while a privately owned system tends to expand the system more aggressively. The Canadian experience has been that, in general, a privately held but state-regulated system has been relatively effective in both directions (as well as being supereffective in a third direction, that of great profitability over long periods of time). The one possible exception may be the beer and liquor monopolies in certain provinces, which enjoy all elements of regulated monopoly except that they don't have to justify their price increases.

Indeed, it seems a waste of time and energy to separate the functions: the system can expand only if the rates allow it, and the rates are driven by how much profit the traffic can bear. In Canada, the system has been immensely profitable to the telephone companies and the consortium of widows who allegedly own most of the telephone stock. It has also produced effective and efficient communication. We can never know if publicly owned systems would have been just as effective in serving the public interest, maximizing profits and keeping the system on the cutting edge of technology while at the same time remaining domestically owned and controlled. The provincially owned telephone companies on the prairies have given mixed indications.

The question of regulated monopolies — and whether the agencies set policy for the companies or the companies set policy for the agencies — is hardly moot today as the telcos are in a battle with the cablecos for control of the information highway's infrastructure. And more than infrastructure is at stake. Cable companies in the United States, often in collaboration with telephone companies and satellite communications systems now merging with giant publishing and production corporations, see themselves as one integrated whole. Some of these agglomerations, like Rupert Murdoch's News Corp. empire, have distinct political agendas in addition to their financial goals. Murdoch has established a satellite news network to compete directly with CNN, in part because of what he (unlike most observers) perceives as CNN's "liberal bias."

The problem with Canada's current regulatory system is that the CRTC's mandate appears to be too broad and, in an increasing number of cases, irrelevant. Former chair Keith Spicer used the CRTC as the proverbial bully pulpit for his notions on sex and violence over the airwaves, seeking to encourage children's television that "concentrates on illustrating values that sensible people of all backgrounds might judge healthy for their children."[10] As well, the commission under his leadership assigned frequencies on some mysterious basis as if satellite and digital transmission did not exist. In one ruling the CRTC replaced an American country music channel with a Canadian one, only to back down when the Americans threatened reprisals.

The Direct-to-Home Satellite Fiasco

Attacking Terence Corcoran, the *Globe and Mail* business columnist whom all readers to the left of Augusto Pinochet love to hate, is easy. Corcoran is too obnoxious in his views to be seen as curmudgeonly, too much the blowhard to be taken seriously even by many of those who agree with him. He rants and raves in his column in a manner often so intemperate as to evoke amazement rather than scorn. But he does sometimes hit the nail on the head in a way that makes sense to people who normally disagree with him, even while approaching a given theme from a contrary ideological bent. Such has been the case in his attacks on the CRTC's stunning botchery of direct-to-home (DTH) satellite television.

In numerous columns on the subject published in 1995 and 1996, Corcoran enjoyed referring to the CRTC as the Canadian Roadblock to Telecommunications Competition. History, it seems, is on his side. For many years, as we have seen, the CRTC blocked attempts to break the lucrative monopoly on long-distance telephone services held by Bell Canada and its sister companies in the Stentor alliance. At least the CRTC was able to come up with logical, if somewhat worn, arguments to support its decisions. But its performance on the DTH issue has been an outright embarrassment.

DTH has been referred to by some fearful broadcasters and cable operators as the "deathstar" because of its ability to deliver vast quantities of signals, eventually up to 500 television channels, to homes that are not even within range of cable services. Naturally, the fact that Canada is a small country with a finite capacity to produce TV programming means that most of these signals would come from foreign sources. Yet the sheer number of these signals would provide room for more programming from overseas, meaning that "foreign" would not translate into "American" quite as automatically as it does now.

Satellite television has been a reality for years in the United States, a market so vast that even a modest level of penetration brings a sizable number of customers. Some of these customers are now found north of the border. Tired of waiting for a legally approved made-in-Canada service, a number of Canadians have bought the requisite equipment and now receive television signals under grey-market arrangements. Some satellite dish dealers estimated the number of Canadian households receiving these services in early 1996 at about 200,000.[11] The reason no Canadian service existed before 1997 was the CRTC's decision, upheld in March 1996 by the federal cabinet, to grant a *de facto* DTH monopoly to a company that apparently lacked either the will or the aptitude to provide such a service in timely fashion.

ExpressVu, this provider, happens to be owned by BCE Inc., with shares held also by Ontario-based Tee-Comm Electronics Corp. and WIC Western International Communications Ltd. of Vancouver in an arrangement brokered by the CRTC. ExpressVu was created in 1993 and, under a CRTC order, was granted an exemption from licensing requirements.[12] General criteria established by the CRTC did, however, require ExpressVu, as well as future competitors, to deliver all signals by Canadian satellites. This in no way conflicted with ExpressVu's business plan. Canada's dominant — and government-coddled — supplier of satellite services is Ottawa-based Telesat Canada Inc. which, since the federal government sold its 53 per cent share in 1992, also happens to be controlled by BCE.[13]

Power Corporation of Canada wanted to get into the DTH business in competition with ExpressVu. Power Corp. is greatly diminished from its glory days of the 1970s, but it still has substantial holdings in the financial services industry. It also owns a small newspaper group whose flagship is *La Presse* of Montreal, and it held a sizable chunk of shares in Southam Inc. until it was bought out by Conrad Black's Hollinger Inc. Power Corp. established a partnership called Power DirecTV in which it owned 80 per cent of the shares, with the remainder held by Los Angeles–based (and at that time General Motors–owned) Hughes Electronics Corp. through its DirecTV subsidiary. Power DirecTV sought to piggyback Canadian programming onto an established U.S. satellite broadcaster. This was to be the Canadian (and mostly Canadian-owned) version of DirecTV, but its business plan called for the use of Hughes's U.S. satellites, causing it to run afoul of CRTC criteria.

When the CRTC did finally grant a licence to Power DirecTV in December 1995, it set terms so onerous that the company decided a few weeks later not to proceed with its plans. The CRTC had relented on the issue of Canadian satellites after the federal cabinet ordered it to promote DTH competition, but it still required DTH providers to carry a full range of specialty services at their own expense, a burden not imposed on the cable companies against which they have to compete.[14] They also must contribute bigger shares of revenues than cable companies to Canadian programming and have to block U.S. signals if a Canadian channel is providing the same programming at the same time. This would mean blocking these U.S. signals to U.S. viewers as well, which is simply not going to happen in the real world. In effect, the CRTC had re-established its earlier prohibition on the use of U.S. satellites.

The CRTC's terms restored ExpressVu's monopoly, but ExpressVu was still not up and running. It had earlier pledged to provide Canadian television viewers with direct-to-home satellite service by September 1995, but this spoiled child of the CRTC missed deadline after deadline and, even after top-level executive changes, it was nowhere close to being in business even a year later.

Such astounding ineptitude is not typical of companies associated with BCE (its huge losses in commercial real estate notwithstanding). However, the monopoly enjoyed by ExpressVu, part of a long Canadian tradition, shows how effectively the CRTC continues to be regulated by powerful companies within its purview. The irony is that this fiasco simultaneously helps BCE's rivals, notably Rogers and the other cable operators. It does this in two ways: it protects their customer base from serious Canadian competition in the immediate future, and ExpressVu's continuing delays allow just enough grey-market penetration by U.S. providers to make the Canadian market less interesting for other would-be DTH operators. We do not normally shed tears for the likes of Power Corp., but the CRTC showed just what it thought of such interlopers. In Terence Corcoran's summation:

> This absurd state of affairs, in which Canadians have no choice but to buy a bootleg U.S. service, is a function of nothing more than trade protectionism, monopoly behaviour and regulatory favouritism. The RCA dishes that Canadians are now buying by the thousands could have been Canadian dishes, sold legally across the country, and offering Canadian programming through a Canadian company. ...
> Now that the Canadian regulatory framework is a shambles, government and industry players are busy trying to create a new framework. Once again, the old back-room power games are being played, the old media scams are being worked, and the same old Canadian consumer is being left out in the cold — and in the dark.[15]

One need not be a Terence Corcoran, all bristle and free-market dogma, to see that something is badly wrong here. Relatively temperate business commentators, such as Jay Bryan of the Montreal *Gazette*, see some obvious value in enhancing access to Canadian content. Tax-funded support for Canadian productions and requirements for would-be importers of foreign programming such as Power DirecTV have been suggested to pay a portion of revenues into a Canadian production fund. Like many other observers, though, Bryan laments the protectionist vision of Keith Spicer's CRTC.

It's this vision that has made cable television companies the government's preferred television gatekeepers and the most hated companies in Canada. It turns them into the CRTC's partners in a corrupt deal that gives them the regulatory green light to gouge consumers so long as they restrict U.S. content while foisting on their viewers the CRTC-approved cable channels that do such a fine job of keeping us aware of important trends in rock videos, weather and Disney movies.

For those who care about Canadian culture, there could be alternatives to this pathetic regime.... But any such alternative would destroy the monopoly power and profits of the cable industry, the CRTC's cherished partner in this game of cultural protectionism. That's why ... the CRTC has made a mockery of the federal government's order that it should facilitate competition in the cable television business....

CRTC restrictions mean that even [ExpressVu] will be unable to compete on price. Result: [Canadian] satellite broadcasting will be a high-priced monopoly of interest only to those who can't get cable....

Of course, there's another result that Spicer and his cronies might not have considered. Destroying the prospect of lower prices and better programming by stifling competition in the cable industry, they have ensured that hundreds of thousands who could have been customers of a truly competitive Canadian satellite broadcast service will now buy the all-American version instead....

That's about $100 million a year in payments going to the all-U.S. services that could have gone to a quality Canadian service. As the satellite market increases to its potential of one million Canadians, this lost opportunity may wind up siphoning $500 million a year out of Canada, hurting consumers and television producers alike and leaving most Canadians prisoners of lousy, overpriced cable service. Thanks, Mr. Spicer.[16]

This situation began to change with the emergence of Canadian DTH service in 1997, but the CRTC and the federal cabinet came out of this débâcle looking decidedly lame. What we see here is the paradoxical effect of too much influence being worse than none at all. Power Corp. is controlled by Paul Desmarais and his two sons, one of whom happens to be married to Prime Minister Chrétien's daughter. The Desmarais clan cherishes its long and close links with both the federal and Quebec Liberal parties. Federal Finance Minister Paul Martin is a former Power Corp. officer. Conflict-of-interest rules may have (or at least ought to have) precluded both the prime minister and the finance minister, the two most powerful members of cabinet, from taking part in cabinet discussions on the DTH issue. Their remaining colleagues may also have wanted to bend over backwards not to be seen favouring Power Corp. interests. Thus connections at the highest levels can be self-defeating.

In the end, the importance of DTH has probably been blown out of proportion. DTH subscribers must buy expensive equipment that may be useless if they wish to switch to a different signal provider. This, along with far from negligible monthly fees, is a major deterrent that is likely to maintain the number of subscribers at modest levels. And DTH cannot offer the same broad scope for interactive services that traditional cable television potentially holds, something that may become especially valuable to the many households that are linked to cable but do not possess home computers or Internet links. But one of the big advantages of DTH from a public policy standpoint is that it can provide competition to the monopoly suppliers of cable television service. Competition tends to mean lower prices, more variety and better service. What we see here is a glaring example of the CRTC chasing a chimera at the expense of sound public policy.

Canadian nationalists may protest that a CRTC-style regime assures Canadian viewers of access to Canadian content, providing at least some measure of Canadian cultural sovereignty. We will not take issue here with the idea that much in the Canadian experience and the Canadian way of seeing things deserves to be treated as something more than a few random multidigit numbers on some future channel selector. Nor do we accept the notion that whatever fails to "compete" in crass commercial terms should be left to die. What we do argue is that some approaches work and some do not.

Let us assume nearly everyone agrees Canadians should produce programming for television and for future forms of communication that exist only in some fertile imagination. Everyone also agrees that Canadians should have ready access to this programming and that audiences abroad should get it as well. Do we achieve this by coddling a handful of favoured monopolists? Do we meet these simple goals by insisting that BCE-controlled satellites are in some way morally superior to GM-controlled satellites?

There exist more promising paths for public policy than CRTC-style restrictions on who can offer what to whom and on whose facilities this content can be transmitted. It has not always seemed clear that the CRTC knows how to tell the difference between content and infrastructure (to be fair, it is not alone in this: in the corporate world, such distinctions are deliberately glossed over and indeed regarded as undesirable). Too often, content has been held hostage to the limitations of infrastructure. Now, however, newish technologies such as digital radio, DTH satellite broadcasting and higher-compression cable television signals spell an imminent end to the scarcity of airwaves that has served to justify a capricious and sometimes obtuse system of regulation in the broadcasting field.

Infrastructure is becoming less of a constraining factor as time goes on, and this is happening without public bodies having to make huge financial or regulatory commitments. The private sector can, and should be allowed to, put in place the infrastructure on its own. But there are public policy considerations and a role for government as well. Under market conditions in Canada, competition policy must be honed to make sure that rival infrastructure providers can enter the field and that those who control infrastructure do not have a stranglehold on content as well. The imminent multiplication of channels, and with it the growing need to fill air time, may actually assure that virtually all programming gets aired — without any public body having to step in.

This brings us to the question of Canadian content, which has been a constant preoccupation of the CRTC, and not without reason. When Canadians began to be swamped by American programming in the fifties, most public policy advisers considered it imperative to ensure that Canadians also had access to a certain minimum of Canadian programming, to the chagrin of private broadcasters. There was no guarantee anyone would watch very much of it apart from hockey games and local news, but they wanted it at least to be available, and this concern has lasted to the present day. (There are Canadian content regulations as well for music on the radio, particularly on the French side where CRTC rules require that a certain portion of songs must be in French.)

New technologies and new realities do not call into question the need for Canadian content, however this concept may be defined, but they do call into question the old ways of enforcing it. Restricting access to foreign programming long ago ceased to be a realistic option. The 500-channel universe will obviously have room for a certain number of Canadian channels. A bigger problem may lie in stimulating the demand. We can bring Canadian programming to Canadian audiences, but will they watch it? Charles Sirois and Claude Forget suggest that in setting criteria for the public funding of Canadian programming it may be the demand side rather than the supply of such material that needs propping up. At the same time, supply cannot be totally ignored: extra consideration may have to go to programming that meets specialized needs even if audiences are likely to be slim.[17]

The Continuing Need for Government Involvement

Ted Rogers, as he builds his cable monopoly at the very hub of Canada's information and communication system, takes the CRTC and government regulation very seriously indeed. He needs the blessing of the federal government to hold the telephone companies with their fibre optic technology at bay. Rogers and his banks are betting an enormous amount of money that the CRTC will protect them. Indeed this faith that government regulations will save the cable industry and preserve its monopoly is manifest in the money willing purchasers are paying for cable monopolies. For example, Rogers is selling Maclean Hunter's cable assets in the United States for approximately $2,400 per subscriber. In Canada, asset swaps and outright purchases are creating three regional cable behemoths — Rogers, Shaw and Vidéotron — and the price for these arrangements is in the same range. Even so, the highly leveraged Rogers faces some serious problems. According to Terence Corcoran, "Even as a large company controlling 40 percent of the Canadian cable-television market, there is reason to doubt that Rogers can survive — unless the cable companies receive continuing protective support from the CRTC."[18]

The decisions of the CRTC and the federal communications bureaucracy pose an increasing menace to the viability of the Canadian state. At least this is how the economics editor of the *Toronto Star*, David Crane, sees it. Reporting on a conference devoted to growing harmonization, really integration, with the United States, Crane connected national survival to the growth of our economic capacity. Citing "Ottawa's foot dragging on the information highway" and its protection (so far) of the cable consortiums against the telephone interests, Crane argued that the government is undermining "its future technology and wealth-creating capacity":

> But if Canada fails to improve its wealth creating capacity through an innovative economy, it cannot improve the standard of living of Canadians; nor can it generate the tax revenues for a Canadian way of life. And if it cannot do those things it cannot sustain the political federation. This is even a greater threat to the Canadian way of life than the threat of harmonization from the United States.

Crane's belief that a government-supported innovative and dynamic domestic capitalist system is the key to an independent future is well developed in his book *The Next Canadian Century*, which has been largely ignored.[19] But one does not have to be a true believer in corporate deliverance to realize the validity of Crane's approach at least in this instance. The information highway will run either through Canada or over it. And how this happens is as much a public issue as was the National Policy, the construction of the east–west transportation system or the building of the national information and communication system.

Information Technology and the Global Economy

Whatever the new information technologies may promise in the future, their effect so far has largely been to increase insecurity, meanness and fear. The information highway challenges social stability at a number of points. First, it destabilizes employment, eliminating some jobs outright by replacing people with machines. Second, it shrinks distance so that other jobs can be moved to low-wage areas. Third, by making borders more penetrable than ever before, it also destabilizes the capacity of societies, organized into nation-states, to implement the decisions they make. More specifically, it destabilizes public finances by making it possible to move vast amounts of money instantly across borders.

The destabilizing force of the new technologies is intensified by the economic ideology currently dominant in the western world: classical liberalism. According to proponents of this ideology, the development of the inforoute has to be left to the "free market." If public authorities attempt to interfere, they will only inhibit innovation, entrepreneurship and creativity. On one level, the technology and the ideology are a good match for each other. The technology makes it more difficult for the state to act effectively, while the ideology says that inaction is not only the easy course but also the right one. But such arguments provide little comfort for a Canadian whose job is automated out of existence or transferred to Asia.

The weakening of the nation-state, brought on by technology and ideology, is the subject of a growing literature. Economist Robert Heilbroner identified it as one of "two formidable self-generated problems" facing contemporary capitalism (the other is the limit to growth implied in ecological barriers):

> The internationalizing tendency of capital ... continues to outpace the defensive powers of individual governments. Thus

capital itself encroaches on the political independence of nations…. Some highly adaptive capitalisms may cope with these problems more effectively than others. But these malfunctions require a transnational political counterforce, and nothing of the kind exists.[1]

The Economist also waded into the fray with a section dealing with the "Myth of the Powerless State,"[2] and frankly couldn't make up its editorial mind. Be that as it may, powerlessness is a relative thing. Some states are more powerless than others. Indeed, not only is the state (even the Canadian state) not powerless, but despite its history of ineptitude it is the only institution that can direct the construction of the information highway and ensure that the new Canadian economy is firmly affixed on it.

The state's involvement does nothing to diminish the need for a transnational structure that can rein in the anarchy implicit in most of the projections and prognostications concerning the new global economy. While no such structures appear to be on the horizon at this point, a wide range of economists, social scientists, business leaders and philosophers see the uncontrolled technological rush and the renewed infatuation with eighteenth- and nineteenth-century laissez-faire ideology as a looming disaster. A modern — or even postmodern — economy cannot function solely on an interpretation or misinterpretation of Adam Smith.

The state needs to rise to meet the challenge of the new economy, both acting individually and through a new economic and social order transcending the narrow, temporary and ultimately destructive interests of corporate shareholders. Unless it does so, society will continue to react to scientific and technological change inappropriately and unwisely. For the moment, however, the argument that we must either "go with the flow" or try vainly to get off the vehicle of progress has the upper hand. The ideology behind this argument is neoconservatism, which also proposes a weakening of social controls and an elimination of the concept of the public interest. It comes to us in the form of U.S. House Speaker Newt Gingrich's "Contract with America" or Ontario Premier Mike Harris's "Common Sense Revolution." The advocates of neoconservatism who brought about "the Reagan Revolution" are now promoting the information highway, of which Gingrich, who had a brief moment in the spotlight as leader of this phase of the revolution, is an enthusiastic supporter:

Maybe we need a tax credit for the poorest Americans to buy a laptop. Now maybe that's wrong, maybe it's expensive, maybe we can't do it. But [it's a] signal we can send to the poorest Americans that says, "We're going into a twenty-first century, third wave information age, and so are you, and we want to carry you with us."

Gingrich is a close friend of Alvin and Heidi Toffler and contributed a foreword to the 1995 edition of their book *Creating a New Civilization: The Politics of the Third Wave.* He apparently takes most of the Tofflers' "third wave" futurism very seriously, especially the stuff about the future "information society" — which in one form or another has become one of the all-purpose yet undefinable clichés of the period.

New Technologies and Social Upheaval

Social commentators from Peter Drucker to Jeremy Rifkin have made the connection between the revolution in communications and the global economy. Defining what he means by his label "The Age of Social Transformation," Drucker argues, in the first instance, that this age — our age — will continue well into the first decades of the next century. It will be an era of "continuing social, economic and political turmoil," one that demands the rethinking and reconstruction of the philosophy and practical understanding of education, all forms of organizational structures such as schools, hospitals, businesses and government, and much else.

Increasingly, says Drucker, the "policy of any country — and especially any developed country — will have to give primacy to the country's competitive position in an increasingly competitive world economy.... The same holds true for the policies and strategies of any institution within a nation, whether a local government, a business, a university or a hospital."[3] While Drucker does not appear to go as far as writers who consider the nation-state an irrelevant anachronism, he does argue that in the new information age the state and all the social organisms within it will drastically change in form and function.

Just what form these changes might take is suggested in a September 1995 survey in *The Economist.* The magazine relates the resurgence of business and industry in the United States to the new information technologies and to structures favourable to the adoption of those technologies, often at the expense of jobs:

America has not only invested more in information technology than any other country; it is also friendlier than most towards organizational experiment. Its market-oriented capitalism is well-suited to the adoption of new productivity-boosting technologies. Its workers are mobile, and its employers have remarkably little compunction about laying people off. Though wretched for discarded workers, this is a blessing for managers keen to change the shape of their firms to take advantage of the new technology.

The Economist goes on to suggest that one principal reason for the resurgence of American business has been massive deregulation, which forced mainly the service industries — banks, airlines and telecommunications companies — to use the new information technology to cope with the competition thus unleashed:

The results have included huge banking mergers, the failure of half a dozen airlines and big job losses in retailing and telecoms....
   Underpinning all of this is something distinctive in American society and politics. No other rich country gives companies such a free hand to lay off workers and shift resources from declining industries into growing ones. No other country refreshes itself in quite the same way by continuous waves of immigration. Bill Miller, professor of management and computer science at Stanford University, describes the special characteristic of American business as a "willingness to reinvent itself and a willingness to see things disappear."... For as long as Americans are willing to put up with the mass layoffs and accompanying social dislocation, these are incomparable wealth-creating advantages.[4]

There are a number of areas to pursue in these quotations from Drucker and *The Economist*. For example, consider the contrast between the "wealth-creating advantages" — the soaring profit ratios of corporate America — and the poverty, cutbacks, deficits and diminution of all the public services and social welfare projects that the United States could easily afford in the 1950s and 1960s — a time when by any objective measure it was a much poorer and economically more primitive society. Or consider the social dislocation manifest in the consciously created urban blight that threatens to reduce Canadian urban centres to the rubble of American ones, which have already been sacrificed to the "incomparable wealth-creating advantages." Thus, the battle between the Harris government and the cities in Ontario, which has focused on the creation of the so-called megacity in Toronto, is primarily about the offloading of social costs — welfare, public housing, urban transportation and other amenities on which the cities depend — so that Queen's Park can cut provincial taxes across the board. The major cities will have only two options: either to raise taxes and thus accelerate the rush to the suburbs or to let the social and even the physical infrastructure deteriorate.

But the area that deserves the closest examination is the end of work and the class that does it — the working class.

The Destruction of Jobs

"No class in history," writes Drucker, "has ever risen faster than the blue collar worker. And no class has fallen faster." Drucker, like many others, goes on to chronicle the rise, and what he sees as the quick and brutal fall, of the industrial worker: "By the year 2000 or 2010, in every developed free-market country, industrial workers will account for no more than an eighth of the work force."[5]

Jeremy Rifkin, the author of *The End of Work: The Decline of the Global Labour Force and the Dawn of the Post Market Era*, has noted that in the 1994 American election, pollsters found "that the real cause fuelling voter unrest [was a] deeper fear ... that an enormous shift is taking place in the economy and millions of Americans are beginning to worry that there may not be a place for them in the new high-tech Information Age."[6]

To date this fear is justified, indeed fuelled, as industry after industry "downsizes," eliminating whole categories of employees. Public-service layoffs and threats of layoffs are defended on grounds that private industry has already established this process. Rifkin writes that blue-collar workers of all descriptions are being eliminated along with secretaries, receptionists, clerical workers, sales clerks, bank tellers, telephone operators, librarians, wholesalers and middle managers. But in ironic testimony to the job-destroying characteristics of the new technology, the only claim not made is that current levels of employment are necessary to maintain current levels of service.

The free market may well be an efficient means of producing goods, but it also destroys jobs — or to be more accurate is unconcerned with all things extraneous to production. Yet even if the individual is reduced to being a mere consumer in a larger model or economic equation, jobs are the issue. Matthew Barrett, chair of the Bank of Montreal, worries how "the new economy will produce enough new jobs to ensure social stability.... [To create a] Darwinian cyber-jungle is not in the self-interest of those of us privileged to have good jobs."[7]

During the week in late 1995 when the Dow Jones industrial average broke 5,000, American Telephone and Telegraph announced buyout offers to 78,000 employees and its stock rose 4 per cent. A few months earlier, when it announced it was splitting into three companies and laying off 8,500 employees, its stock rose 10 per cent. When the Royal Bank of Canada announced its own record-breaking profit — the profit record for Canadian banks is broken every quarter — it also announced a layoff of 1,000 employees.

There are a number of parallels in these developments. AT&T, which is in control of or in partnership or alliance with the essential players in the creation of the infrastructure of the information highway (the telcos and cablecos), is both downsizing and expanding its operations. The Royal Bank claimed that its profit rise was due mainly to service charges at its ATMs and telebanking services — those elements of the banking system most closely connected to the development of computer and communication technology. And the story repeats itself throughout the vast web of interconnected industries: technological change means higher profits but fewer and fewer jobs.

In a sense this was always the case. Technological change always eliminates jobs. On the other hand, in the past new ones have been found, usually better ones with higher wages and better prospects. Jobs are lost, but efficiencies increase production — more and different goods and services are created. Earlier industrial revolutions, where potential workers fled or were driven from the farms to the industrial cities, caused serious dislocation and suffering for many people. But eventually things sorted themselves out, and however unevenly it was distributed, the new wealth that was created was indeed a tide that lifted all boats.

One side of this classical equation is certainly operating as the model predicts: employment in established industries is decreasing. In some industries, such as textiles and steel, there has been an absolute decline in both production and employment. In the auto industry, although more and more cars are being produced, the number of workers needed to produce them is declining. In the United States, for example, where the newly energized Big Three are taking back their market share and demanding a growing chunk of the Japanese and European markets, membership in the United Automobile Workers union has shrunk from 1.5 million to 800,000.

And so, with the classical model in mind, people are being urged to draw the obvious lessons: learn about the new technology, develop new skills, train, retrain, and get as much education as possible. Don't get stuck with the group that will be left behind as the old economy dies or moves to the Third World, which is now being incorporated into the new global economy. But the other half of the tradeoff between job loss and productive growth — declining prices — has not worked out. Automobile prices rise every year, and new and more exotic bank service charges proliferate. Indeed, this imbalance between trends in employment and prices may help explain the somewhat curious observation that the smaller a corporation becomes, the more profitable it is. The holy dividend, or even the promise of one, entices the investor. Allan Sloan wrote in *Newsweek* in November 1995:

> News of layoffs levitates your stock. The rationale: layoffs will one day mean higher profits, justifying a higher stock price today. So if you're a typical corporate-employee type who owns stocks or mutual funds, you can't wait to see the news and find out if a new round of layoffs has made money for you. You just hope to God that your company isn't the one making the announcement.[8]

So this typical corporate-employee type with investments wins on one bet and loses on the other. But if you are the even more typical corporate-employee type who relies completely on his or her job and wage, you have only one bet on the table, and it is a losing one.

Unemployment and the Dislocation of Workers

Another way to approach the long-term effect of technology on jobs is to look at unemployment statistics. Unemployment is supposed to rise and fall with the business cycle, but in addition to these cyclical variations the statistics show a slow but steady increase in joblessness as technology allows companies to produce more using fewer workers.

To be sure, these statistics are notoriously understated and unreliable. In Canada, for example, fewer than 50 per cent of the unemployed are currently eligible for employment insurance, there are few data on how many people have simply been removed from the labour force, and no one seems willing to correlate unemployment with the rapidly increasing welfare rolls as the so-called jobless recovery stalls. Nevertheless, even the official statistics indicate a trend. During the prosperous sixties, the unemployment rate hovered around 4 per cent. In the even more prosperous early and middle 1980s, it averaged around 8 per cent. With the recovery of the early 1990s — even before it "paused," in the words of Finance Minister Paul Martin — unemployment did not fall below 9 per cent.

Mass unemployment has become a phenomenon of the developed industrial countries that are leading the way to the new economic age. Industrialized Europe suffers high and unyielding rates of unemployment. France, for example, has a seemingly permanent rate of around 12 per cent. Moving over to Germany, Rifkin cites a chilling comparison made by former chancellor Helmut Schmidt between unemployment rates now and in the 1930s: "More people are unemployed in Chemnitz, Leuna or Frankfurt than in 1933, when people there elected the Nazis."[9]

The only exception in the Western world is the current level of between 5 and 6 per cent unemployment in the United States. But the United States is where the term "working poor" originated — nearly 60 per cent of Americans who fall below the poverty line are in families in which at least one person has full-time or part-time work.

The United States is also where presidential hopefuls such as Pat Buchanan claim that the 20 per cent decline in purchasing power of the average American family over the past two decades and the destruction of the "American Dream" are caused by foreigners, high taxes and generous welfare to unappreciative and lawless blacks. As long as Buchanan was acting out his racist, misogynist bigotry he was dismissed as at best an articulate populist and at worst a loose cannon on the political right who threatened the more respectable folk in the Republican Party by speaking out what they think. But when Buchanan widened his attack on the leadership of industrial and financial America, denouncing the "corporate greed" that had led to the loss of American jobs, he won a primary and slipped beyond the pale. When he carelessly spoke about peasants with pitchforks marching on the castles, the court jester was no longer funny. The candidate who four years earlier had proclaimed a cultural civil war to cheering Republicans suddenly became a nonperson. All he needed was a tiny dollop of truth in a sea of demagogy and the star of the political talk shows was out in the cold.

If unemployment is used not as a gauge but as a harbinger of recession, then the business cycle is becoming ever shorter. We are now down to an interval of five years between recessions, if a recession is defined as two consecutive quarters of GDP decline. At the same time, what stage of the cycle we are in is becoming somewhat irrelevant. A recession now primarily means an aggravation of the now constant phenomenon of high unemployment. A recent study by the Organization for Economic Cooperation and Development noted that longer-term unemployed in the U.S. (over fifteen weeks) now constitute more than 12 per cent of the jobless. This figure has been rising at an ever-accelerating rate for the past fifteen years, even allowing for all the business-cycle fluctuations during that period.[10]

Rifkin has concluded that within thirty years the industrialized countries will be dealing with unemployment rates of 80 per cent, with an elite 20 per cent secure in jobs in the knowledge and entertainment industries. An even more alarmist prediction appears in a study from the Geneva-based International Metalworkers Federation asserting that the march of technology means that in thirty years as little as 2 per cent of the world's current labour force will suffice to meet total industrial demand.

This process has been somewhat obscured by the fact that the basis of the American economic recovery lies partly in the export of manufactured goods, something that in bygone days was less of an American priority. In Canada, the Ontario comeback — such as it is, or more precisely was — is based on such "new age" technologies as the automobile, which has lessened the impact of increasing lay-offs in telecommunications, electronics, management and services. The recovery in British Columbia and Alberta is almost totally re-source-based. But how long will it last? Whatever economists may disagree on, there is little doubt on one question: the mere export of nonrenewable resources does not make a modern economy — just as the assembly of parts and vehicles is, at least as far as labour is concerned, a "mature" and shrinking part of the total design and production process.

The shift is to what Drucker calls the "knowledge worker." This will not be an easy transition: to become a knowledge worker requires education. Even more pertinently, the need for knowledge workers is also diminishing. Many of the victims of current massive layoffs in such industries as computers and telecommunications are precisely the vaunted knowledge workers. AT&T, IBM and Digital Equipment Corporation have been among the most prominent job cutters. Unemployment and job instability are far from being limited to the seasonal, low-wage and depressed areas and rotting city cores. In the arc surrounding Toronto — known as "905" after its telephone area code — economic uncertainty has provided fertile ground for the politics of meanness exemplified by Premier Mike Harris. Here we are talking not only about the harried hamburger flipper juggling two or three jobs but also about the highly educated, trained and retrained "contractor" or "consultant" who moves ever more dispiritedly from temporary contract to temporary contract. These people tend not to be reflected in most jobless statistics, but they are a growing segment of the labour force.

This brings us back to our question: where is the new economy? In Bangalore, India; mainland China; even Ireland. The telecommunications revolution has, as they say, eliminated distance. In a special survey on telecommunications, *The Economist* asks what it will be like "when the cost of communications comes down to next to nothing."[11]

Already, the first glimpses of this world are beginning to appear. India has built a flourishing computer-software industry around Bangalore. It is also attracting back-office work from companies such as Swissair and British Airways. Some of Hong Kong's paging services are staffed from well inside China. In Perth, in Western Australia, EMS Control Systems monitors the air conditioning, lighting, elevators and security in office blocks in Singapore, Malaysia, Sri Lanka, Indonesia and Taiwan. Telecom Ireland has been trying to build itself up as the main call centre for Europe, handling toll free 0800 calls from all over the continent. In Canada, New Brunswick has followed a similar course, basing its economic development strategy on low-wage work that advances in telecommunications have made geographically mobile.

The Economist goes on to make the point that the new mobility of service jobs brought on by the inforoute will expose white-collar workers in rich countries to the same competitive pressures that have already squeezed manufacturing workers. Just how that process works was outlined in a 1995 Conference Board of Canada report quoted by Peter Cook in the *Globe and Mail.*[12] While corporate profits are growing and workers are becoming more productive, real wages in Canada are actually declining. According to the report, the average nonunionized employee in Canada would get a 2.3 per cent pay raise, and the average unionized employee a 1.8 per cent increase. Profits in recent quarters have risen by 30 to 40 per cent.

While profits rise across the economy, the picture in the telecommunications, computer and computer-driven industries is much more complex — incoherent is probably a better word. The only constant appears to be job reductions. Thus, Apple lost $740 million in the first quarter of 1996, and as a reflection of this, it cut 2,800 jobs. In 1997, as part of a desperate — some suggest last-ditch — bid to save the company, Apple laid off another third of its remaining employees. These were mainly contractors. In the 1996 round of cuts, Apple Canada announced layoffs of 25 per cent of its work force as a result of its own first-quarter loss of $69 million. This eliminated a total of forty-five jobs, which says something about the size of Apple Canada in relation to head office. But Canada has its own home-grown job losses as well. The former Northern Telecom, now Nortel with most of its operations and manufacturing outside of Canada, is vacating its nominal head office in Mississauga, laying off about a thousand employees and installing the survivors in one of its empty factories in another Toronto suburb.

But the most interesting and confusing story comes from AT&T. AT&T made the big news of 1996 when it announced that it was separating off several of its parts to concentrate on telephone service. A byproduct of this corporate restructuring was that 40,000 employees would be laid off. This announcement was greeted warmly on Wall Street, which sent AT&T's stock through the roof. When it came to its annual meeting, shareholders were told that in spite of the huge charge against earnings occasioned by the restructuring cost, the company still made more money in the first quarter of 1996 than in the final quarter of 1995. Earnings per share rose to 90 cents from 80 cents and sales from continuing operations of the company increased to $12.96 billion. This would leave plenty of money for AT&T stockholders to invest in the companies being separated off: Lucent Technologies, NCR Corp. and AT&T Capital. All of these companies are profitable.

Meanwhile, inflation was expected to increase by 2.8 per cent and take-home pay would fall in after-inflation terms. Peter Cook attributes the decline largely to the high and ever-growing tax increases necessary to pay down the deficit and to protect the fraying "social safety net." (He doesn't mention the fact that while consumption and marginal tax rates have been rising, corporate taxes have been decreasing, which may in part be responsible for both the decline in take-home pay for workers and the enormous increase in corporate profits.) Another factor, however, is global competition in which everything except labour is mobile and distance has been abolished. As Cook suggests:

With the option of being able to relocate plants or offices to somewhere else where costs are lower, and with a bunch of employees who remain terrified of losing their jobs, those same companies do not need to match productivity gains with pay gains and, by all indications, won't.[13]

Commenting on the report, Prem Benimadhu mentioned a "disconnect" at work. Cook explains: "The connection between corporations making more money, employees being more productive, and corporations passing on pay raises to their employees has somehow been broken."

Also unanswered, even by the proponents of the consumer-driven free market, is the problem of the consumerless society. A dislocated working class is not only "wretched" for the unemployed, but it also makes them nonconsumers. It is estimated, for example, that the world's automobile industry can produce ten million more cars per model year than can possibly be sold. And in North America, where the stock market booms and corporate profits soar, consumer confidence indexes decline. Indeed the analogy can be made between the years of declining consumer purchasing power that presaged the crash of 1929 and today's market. Thus, the amount of work time required to pay for a new car increased by 40 per cent between 1991 and 1997.

To pursue the analogy, it was not simply the industrial revolution of mass production that caused the economic imbalances of the

1920s. It was also the "sound" economics of balanced budgets, price stability and minimal government controls. Similarly, we believe that the current technological revolution is merely part of a new reality. The issue is the social response to this new reality. And so far the response has been rather scary.

This response has taken the form of intense efforts to deregulate, privatize and return government to its pre-1929 impotence. Government, said Ronald Reagan, is not the solution; it is the problem. There is no society, said Margaret Thatcher; there are only individuals. And since nobody has repealed the business cycle, the overwhelming thrust has been to dismantle the instruments that ameliorate it. The 1930s proved that what falls does not necessarily rise of its own accord. That lesson has been ignored.

Computer Networks and Capital Flows

The terms "recession", "recovery" and even "boom" have become more and more meaningless and have been replaced by oxymorons such as "jobless recovery" and "creeping growth." As far back as 1993, Jeremy Brecher summarized "seven danger signals of cancerous, out of control globalization."[14] As each workforce, community or country seeks to become more competitive by reducing its wages and its social and environmental overheads, the result is a general downward spiral in incomes and social and material infrastructure. Lower wages and reduced buying power lead to stagnation, recession and unemployment. This dynamic is aggravated by the accumulation of debt; national economies in poor countries, even in the United States, and especially in Canada become geared to debt repayment at the expense of consumption, investment and development.

According to former U.S. Labor Secretary Robert Reich, "Between 1978 and 1987, the poorest fifth of American families became 8 percent poorer and the richest fifth became 13 percent richer. That means the poorest fifth have less than 5 percent of the nation's income while the richest fifth have more than 40 percent." Reich goes on to state that the fundamental cause of the widening gap "is that America itself is ceasing to exist as an economic unit separate from the rest of the world. One can no more meaningfully speak of an 'American economy' than of a 'Delaware economy.' We are becoming but a region — albeit still a relatively wealthy region — of a global economy."[15]

Along with the declining sense of a national economy comes a declining sense of national community. The late Christopher Lasch wrote that the privileged classes — the top 20 per cent — have cancelled their allegiance to America: "It is not just that they see no need in paying for public services they no longer use; many of them have ceased to think of themselves as Americans in any important sense.... Many members of the elite [are] deeply indifferent to the prospect of national decline."[16] As we noted in Chapter 4, the information highway, with its "virtual communities" that provide escape from one's geographical surroundings not only to the elites but also to those of more modest means, contributes to this process.

Meanwhile, back in the real communities, we struggle with the growing gap between rich and poor — not only within each country but also internationally, as communications technology eases the flow of capital between countries and regions of the globe. Money flowing from South to North in the form of repayments of principal and interest, repatriated profits, capital flight, royalties and fees for patents and information exceeds the amount flowing from North to South by between $40 and $50 billion annually. The United States has been the greatest beneficiary of this imbalance. As Geoffrey Hawthorn noted, "At its peak in 1987, the net resource transfer to the U.S. from the rest of the world was $151 billion."[17] Almost half this money came from the Third World. Recently, with increased capital demands from Europe, it has been left more and more to Asia and Africa to finance the United States.

Everyone seems fixated on the method, not the madness, of the movement of capital through cyberspace — reputedly, a trillion dollars every twenty-four hours. It is all real money and it is going from one pocket to another; somebody is losing it and somebody is gaining it. Ripped out of any context, the instantaneous movement of capital around the globe is insistently described as a new phenomenon and one that is impossible either to regulate or to control.

But since the invention of the telegraph well over a hundred years ago (considered now to be the first element of the information highway), buy, sell and move signals could travel at least in the industrialized world almost at the speed of light. Theoretically, capital has always been mobile, both inside and outside a national market economy, as Adam Smith brilliantly described. America was largely built on foreign capital, which ironically was created through the export of fur and other primitive staples to Britain and continental Europe and then sent back to finance the canals and railways and infrastructure of the North American continent. While it may have taken more time two hundred years ago, capital then as now has always flowed to the source of the immediate highest return and away from danger and depletion.

A 1995 *Economist* survey suggested that before the First World War, the net capital flowing across borders, in relationship to the size of the economies, was actually larger than at present. For example, Britain between 1880 and 1913 ruled not only the waves but also the international capital markets. Governments tried for a time to control capital movements and were often successful. It wasn't until the 1970s, in the wake of the collapse of the Bretton Woods Agreement, that most gave up and abdicated to the market. In 1973 typical daily foreign-exchange trading amounted to between $10 and $20 billion. In 1983 it ranged around $60 billion. The daily turnover in 1996 nudged $1.3 trillion on a dull to average trading day.

Capital has always been moved internationally. The ebb and flow of this movement has been controlled not by technology but by political decision. The real difference is the volume and speed: $1.3 trillion moving about in cyberspace at any time (as compared to less than $700 billion in total foreign currency reserves of all the governments of the industrialized world combined) and the speed with which it can be moved amount to a potential crisis looking for a place to happen.

Mexico is a classic case in point. There was first a massive flow of capital into Mexico. But capital seemed to flow out even faster than in. Mexico ran a current accounts deficit until in 1994 it averaged around 8 per cent of GDP. In December 1994, the banks decided to call in Mexico's loans and the peso dropped precipitously. "The markets simply lost their heads," *The Economist* concluded. But that is somewhat beside the point. It is not the whys and wherefores that matter but the fact that it can happen — that a country can be virtually bankrupted by the flick of a digit on a keyboard.

The once irresistible magnet was cut off: that was the easy part. Then the banks had to be bailed out and all the speculators and finally the American and the Canadian government had to guarantee the bailouts — all political decisions made by human beings quite independent of the omnipotent computer. Capital can move with a flick of a switch and it can be stopped from moving with another flick of the same switch. It can also be directed. There is computer trading and the computers can get out of control, creating the effect suffered by the sorcerer's apprentice in *Fantasia*. But computers are programmed by human beings making deliberate decisions. If this were not the case, measures such as the so-called Tobin Tax, a proposed small levy on currency transactions to dampen the effects of speculation, would simply be dismissed as impossible rather than being vigorously opposed as undesirable.

The new technology has contributed to the reckless speed that seems to be a required element of the new global economy. It has also created the illusion that the economy operates not only beyond any government's control but beyond human control. This lack of control has helped generalize frustrating feelings of uncertainty and powerlessness. Governments (or some of them) have largely abandoned their regulatory powers for ideological and political reasons that have nothing to do with the technological imperatives of the electronic information system.

For example, in the fall of 1994, seventeen of the world's largest central banks threw more than $5 billion into the market in one trading session to prop up the American dollar. It had absolutely no effect on the trillion-dollar-a-day global currency market. According to Thomas L. Friedman, the banks were like "a zoo keeper trying to calm a starved gorilla by offering it a raisin for lunch."[18] It now turns out, however, that the American dollar falls because the Federal Reserve wants it to — the falling dollar puts the United States in a better competitive position with Europe and especially Japan, as it raises the prices of imported goods on the American market and lowers the prices of American goods on the world market. In addition, a falling dollar lowers American interest rates, which is supposed to spark the economy. This is the theory, at least, and since the Federal Reserve subscribes to this theory it has other uses for its relatively limited supply of raisins.

The money moves literally with the speed of light. That's the information highway. There are no limits. And no one to enforce them if there were. Or at least, so it would appear.

Life Without Jobs?

There is also another edge to the globalization of markets that is evident from global resource transfers. In a 1995 speech in Ontario, Lester Thurow noted that while capital markets remain in New York and prices are set there, technology is global and the current gap between the developed world and the newly industrialized countries will be short-lived. The globalization of markets for goods and services has already meant that most Canadian and American workers must expect continued declines in real income.

If you're a North American worker, you're competing with the Koreans. Like you, they borrow in New York and get their technology in global markets. The cost of raw materials declines in real terms year in and year out, and the ready availability of these resources used to be your edge. The Koreans are better educated than you are, so you must expect to be working for Korean wages or less.[19]

This puts in context Newt Gingrich's opposition to increasing the minimum wage in the United States as it will hurt American workers in competition for jobs with Mexican workers. It also puts in context a 1995 editorial in *The Economist* to the effect that the humbling of the British trade union movement has meant that it is now cheaper to hire workers in Britain than elsewhere in Europe: "Britain has no minimum wage (at least until Labour takes office) which would add to unemployment by stopping firms hiring people who would work for less than that minimum."[20] It also puts in some context the Ontario Tories' aversion to the increase in minimum wages when they were in opposition and their determination once in power to repeal the previous NDP government's amendments to the Labour Relations Act.

The heart and soul of the new Tory labour legislation in Ontario, and one of the major issues in the Ontario public service strike of early 1996, was the renunciation of successor rights of unions. If, for example, the Ontario government wanted to sell off a bureau, or even whole activities and departments of the civil service (say licence bureaus), the existing employees, including their union, used to be part of the package. No more. Thus, what is now a labour-intensive operation with relatively well-paid workers could easily be privatized by being contracted out to a highly computerized specialty operation. No union, no workers.

In the strike, the Ontario Public Service Employees Union (OPSEU) was not able to save successor rights since the change occurred through legislation and not through negotiations. However, OPSEU did gain a promise that the government would use its best efforts to assure the same wages and conditions from the private sector. While that doesn't mean much in itself, any civil servant facing a significant drop in wages as a result of privatization can refuse the job and qualify for a severance package. This provision will make it more expensive for the government to sell off sections of the public service. The agreement also expanded the right of laid-off employees to bump others with lower seniority, which will further complicate actual layoffs.

Similar practices have been developing for years in the private sector. In October 1995, the *Globe and Mail* ran a photograph of a Toronto woman working on a computer in what looks to be the bedroom closet of a cramped apartment. She is an employee of Pizza Pizza, a large pizza delivery chain, and her function is to take and dispatch pizza orders. And she is one of the lucky ones. She is unionized and makes $7 an hour. After a long and bitter strike, most Pizza Pizza order takers are no longer part of the union. These nonunion order takers must rent their computers and receive only 25 cents a call. But according to the *Globe and Mail*, there is another catch: "Sooner or later both groups will be out of a job entirely. Another chain ... has begun taking orders on the Internet and plans to bypass order-takers altogether."[21]

From pizza to government, the process is the same: the replacement of relatively secure, unionized, full-time work with casual part-time work. It is easy for the employers but disastrous for workers and civil society in general. As one of the studies presented to the Information Highway Advisory Council states, "Canadian workers find themselves squeezed closer to the economic margins and facing an increasingly uncertain future."

There are answers to these questions about the future of employment from the various governments, industry gurus and studies — some vacuous and others more so. For example, the *Globe and Mail* quotes Industry Canada as reporting that "less work in the future is not a disaster but an opportunity. People should think not of jobs, which will be increasingly scarce as well as costly and difficult to create, but of incomes, which can come in different ways."

Of course, this kind of talk is not new. The idea and prospect of automation (an old-fashioned but more accurate term than the clumsy notion of knowledge and information industries) have been around since the dawn of the industrial age. The prospect has always been met with predictions of the "leisure society" — a term that has gone out of the lexicon along with "full employment." And it is clear enough that as machines do more and more work, people have to do less and less.

But the needs in people's lives that have been filled through their jobs — from income and financial security to personal fulfilment, camaraderie and social solidarity — do not go away. No doubt there are other ways of meeting those needs, and looking for those new

ways is a more productive response to the current situation than
pining for the days of guaranteed manufacturing jobs from high
school graduation to retirement. What is clear, however, is that such
solutions are not going to be found solely in the context of the "free
market."

Even the Information Highway Advisory Council acknowledged
the "need for labour legislation to adapt labour standards to the new
environment and provide protection to workers in non-traditional
arrangements equivalent to the protection enjoyed by those working
in more traditional settings."[22] But this was as far as the business-ori-
ented majority on the council was willing to go. It favoured a "market-driven" approach to employment questions and pronounced itself
"wary" of international social charters as a means of promoting
equity and justice in the workplace.

This unwillingness to consider any measures even remotely com-
mensurate with the scale of the social dislocation that Western societies face provoked an open split on the council, leading the labour
representative, Canadian Labour Congress executive vice-president
Jean-Claude Parrot, to issue a minority report. The council majority's
package of recommendations on employment issues, Parrot said,
"falls short of what Canadian workers need and deserve," and he
maintained that "market-driven solutions to unemployment clearly
do not work."[23]

In addition to viewing international social charters more favour-
ably, Parrot also took a more expansive view of the kinds of measures
governments should take. These included proposals to "require firms
that undertake large-scale layoffs to use all available and agreed-to
methods of mitigating job losses such as work-sharing, shortened
working hours, and utilization of telework options" and to "require
the mandatory provision of employment and workplace impact statements from firms which apply for federal regulatory approval, tax
incentives or other financial assistance for the development of Information Highway initiatives."[24] But limited and far from utopian proposals such as these appear to face insurmountable obstacles in the
current ideological climate.

Author and scientist Ursula Franklin, who has studied the social
impact of technological change for many years, sees technology as
"an agent of power and control":

> Since the 1800's when the industrial revolution got underway,
> we knew that the explicit purpose of inventing machines and

devices was, ultimately, to reduce the need for human beings, who get sick or go on strike. That's why owners want more technology.... It gives them greater control of their operations.[25]

Dr. Franklin has cited the restructuring of work as one of her particular fears about technological change: "More and more people are losing meaningful work."[29]

And then there is the old story of Henry Ford showing United Auto Workers President Walter Reuther some new assembly machines — this was even before robots.

"How are you going to get union dues from these fellas?" Ford asked.

"How are you going to sell them cars?" Reuther replied.

Inforoute Anxiety

The information highway has created, in large measure, the conditions for the existence and development of the global economy. The relationship between the inforoute and the new economy is analogous to the relationship between the steam engine — the technological harbinger of the first industrial revolution — and the development of the free market, although the current change is perhaps even more profound. Previous industrial revolutions were exactly that: industrial, in that they affected mainly industry. The current revolution affects not only industry but also politics, society and culture — from communication to arts and science, from the systems that control the assembly-line robots and the image transferrals that enable remote-controlled operations, through interactive banking and financial transfers, to unscramblers that will access the interactive infinite-channel universe.

The material conditions for the disintegration of the modern industrial state are being created by the technical and industrial revolution represented by the information highway — and by the social and political response to that revolution. There is plenty of historical precedent, from the fall of ancient societies to the rise of industrial capitalism, for social disruption and disintegration following in the wake of economic change. Two aspects of the impact of the information highway, we believe, deserve special attention: its effects on employment and its effects on the nation-state.

In a widely discussed article in the prestigious journal *Foreign Affairs*, Ethan B. Kapstein, Director of Studies at the Council on Foreign Relations, noted that "populists and demagogues of various stripes will find 'solutions' to contemporary economic problems in protectionism and xenophobia.... Such figures are on the campaign trail now."

Kapstein suggested that the "dogma of restrictive fiscal policy" is undermining "the bargain struck with workers in every industrialized country.... States are basically telling their workers they can no longer afford the postwar deal and must minimize their obligations. The current obsession with balanced budgets in the United States and the Maastricht criteria in Europe must be replaced by an equally vigilant focus on growth and equity." He concluded:

> While the world stands at a critical time in postwar history, it has a group of leaders who appear unwilling, like their predecessors in the 1930's, to provide the international leadership to meet economic dislocations. Worse, many of them and their economic advisers do not seem to recognize the profound trouble affecting their societies. Like the German elite in Weimar, they dismiss mounting worker disatisfaction, fringe political movements, and the plight of the unemployed and working poor as marginal concerns compared with the unquestioned importance of a sound currency and balanced budget. Leaders need to recognize the policy failures of the past 20 years and respond accordingly. If they do not, there are others waiting in the wings who will, perhaps on less pleasant terms.[1]

For a brief moment in early 1996, in the United States at least, fear, uncertainty and dislocation appeared to have reached unsustainable levels. There may not have been bread lines and hobo jungles to bring back memories of the 1930s, but there was a political figure, one of Kapstein's "populists and demagogues," who evoked the likes of Huey Long, Father Charles Coughlin and William Aberhart. Pat Buchanan attracted surprising levels of support in the early Republican caucuses and primaries by addressing people's deep-seated economic anxieties. He took a strident America First position, rejected globalization, proposed American withdrawal from the North American Free Trade Agreement and the World Trade Organization, called for a trade policy that "put American workers first," denounced the "corporate greed" that had led to the loss of American jobs, and sought to protect workers from job competition by declaring a moratorium on immigration. But perhaps the most revealing thing about Buchanan was the reaction to him from the mainstream right.

For Terence Corcoran, Buchanan's campaign amounted to "destructive and unprincipled exploitation of social and economic fears. He is, like most populists, a collectivist masquerading as an American individualist. Mr. Buchanan is a dangerous fraud."[2] David Frum was no less concerned by Buchanan's rise, seeing it as a sign that the mainstream right had unwisely ignored the concerns that Buchanan spoke to. Both Frum and Corcoran hastened to link Buchanan with other opponents of free trade: Frum heard echoes of Liberal leader John Turner's 1988 campaign against the Canada–U.S. Free Trade Agreement, while Corcoran placed Buchanan in the company of Canadian Labour Congress president Bob White.

Nor was the backlash against the effects of the free market limited to Buchanan. "CORPORATE KILLERS," screamed the magazine cover. Significantly, three of the four "killers" pictured were the heads of companies in industries closely linked to the information highway: "Robert B. Palmer, Digital, Cut 20,000 jobs; Albert J. Dunlap, Scott, Cut 11,000 jobs; Robert E. Allen, AT&T, Cut 40,000 jobs; Louis V. Gerstner, IBM, Cut 60,000 jobs."[3] Inside, the salaries of these and other chief executive officers who had initiated massive layoffs were featured — $3,362,000 for Allen, $2,625,000 for Gerstner, a relatively modest $900,016 for Palmer. An anachronistic tract from the last vestiges of the old left? Hardly. All this appeared in the February 26, 1996, issue of *Newsweek*. To be sure, the feature article by Wall Street editor Allan Sloan criticized the corporate leaders primarily for insensitivity and bad public relations, rather than for doing anything fundamentally wrong. Nevertheless, it was another indication of the extent to which the theme of out-of-control capitalism causing widespread suffering struck a chord.

Meanwhile, the *International Herald Tribune* ran an essay by two of the top organizers of the World Economic Forum in Davos, Switzerland, described by Thomas L. Friedman of the *New York Times* as "an annual celebration of globalization — that loose combination of free-trade agreements, the Internet and the integration of financial markets that is erasing borders and uniting the world into a single, lucrative, but brutally competitive, marketplace."[4] The title of the essay: "Start Taking the Backlash Against Globalization Seriously."

In 1993, the U.S. government's *National Information Infrastructure: Agenda for Action* asserted that "an advanced information infrastructure will enable U.S. firms to compete and win in the global economy, generating good jobs for the American people and economic growth for the nation."[5] In a similar vein, the Canadian government's Information Highway Advisory Council in its 1995 report justified its free-market approach to technological change on grounds that "competition reinforces a cycle of greater innovation, higher productivity, lower prices, higher quality and greater choice. It lays a new foundation from which all firms, large and small, can grow and create jobs."[6] But rhetoric of this nature has not aged gracefully. Capitalism has begun to recognize the existence of a job crisis, in which technology — especially computer, information and communications technology — is a major element.

Ideas for dealing with the crisis abound. Governments have tended to favour training and adjustment programs, retrofitting workers to match jobs that may or may not exist. Another set of proposals acknowledges that as machines do more work human beings will do less and seeks to distribute the available employment more equitably: shorter work weeks, job sharing, providing fringe benefits for part-time workers to mitigate the disadvantages of nonstandard employment, flexible hours, society-wide sabbatical programs. Such ideas may offer only limited hope to those people who are simply not suited to being high-tech "knowledge workers," and whose prospects for even part-time employment are therefore likely to be increasingly constrained. Yet many of these ideas are well worth exploring. However, governments and corporations have so far shown little appetite for implementing them. Their only answer has been to push ever growing numbers of people into unemployment and the overcrowded bottom of the job market.

As long as managing the employment effects of technological change is left to the "free market," that is the only answer that will ever be offered. People will turn increasingly to advocates of state intervention — "collectivists" such as Pat Buchanan, whether bearing the label of right or left. Buchanan is as abhorrent to us as he is to Terence Corcoran, but his voters have sent a message that needs to be heeded.

Coping with Global Information

Inforoute anxiety reigns in widely scattered places around the world, in locales ranging from Canada's own CRTC to the pervasive government security forces in countries such as Singapore and Vietnam, to name only two of the more forthright would-be blockers of electronic bits. As we saw earlier, the Internet with its World Wide Web and its myriad discussion groups, together with other parts of the inforoute such as satellite-to-home television with its plethora of signals, and even some of their older counterparts ranging from specialty magazines to short-wave radio broadcasts, allow people to join communities that are defined by sometimes arcane interests rather than by national boundaries that took shape many decades or even centuries ago. Are these communities any less legitimate than groups that identify themselves according to the nation-states in which they happen to reside?

Two recent books, coming from different continents and different traditions, both have as their titles in English *The End of the Nation State*.[7] One of the authors is Japanese management consultant Kenichi Ohmae, a former senior partner with the American firm McKinsey and Company; the other is Jean-Marie Guéhenno, a political scientist and former French envoy to the European Union. These divergent backgrounds are reflected in the views they express.

Ohmae is keen on what he calls the four I's — industry, investment, individuals and information — being able to flow relatively unimpeded across the borders of nation-states, which he derides as nineteenth-century building blocks that are losing validity as the twenty-first century approaches:

> Are these nation states — notwithstanding the obvious and important role they play in world affairs — really the primary actors in today's global economy? Do they provide the best window on that economy? Do they provide the best port of access to it? In a world where economic borders are progressively disappearing, are their arbitrary, historically accidental boundaries genuinely meaningful in economic terms? And if not, what kinds of boundaries do make sense?[8]

By posing these questions the way he does, Ohmae leaves little doubt that he regards the answers to all but the last of them as an emphatic no. Ohmae seems to be uncomfortable even mentioning the word *government,* which he appears to equate with *nation-state.* Can nation-states exist without governments? Can governments exist without nation-states? Can international organization exist without either? Some of his fellow globalizers may be content to dispense with both, but Ohmae does have a replacement in mind:

> The qualifications needed to sit at the global table and pull in global solutions begin to correspond not to the artificial political borders of countries, but to the more focused geographical units — Hong Kong, for example, or the Kansai region around Osaka, or Catalonia — where real work gets done and real markets flourish. I call these units "region states."... What defines them is not the location of their political borders but the

fact that they are the right size and scale to be the true, natural business units in today's global economy.[9]

Apart from the implication that work gets done only in certain imaginary "region states," this idea is an interesting one and harks back to the early city-state concept. It would respond to well-justified complaints in many parts of the world about indifference or wrongheadedness from remote central governments, although not necessarily to similar complaints about remote corporate head offices. Where Ohmae disappoints is in his failure to suggest any coherent form of political organization that could reflect the economic and social importance of these region-states.

On the other hand, Jean-Marie Guéhenno starts with the premise that the nation-state forms an essential part of the democratic ideal, and he laments what he regards as its imminent demise.[10] He places the end of the age of nation-states in 1989, the year the Berlin Wall fell and also, incidentally, the bicentennial of the French Revolution, which had given the nation-state idea considerable impetus.

The polarization wrought by the Cold War had given order to human societies, Guéhenno argues, and anti-Communism enabled rulers to put aside questions of political identity.[11] The "spatial society" represented by the nation-state is being replaced by temporary interest groups; borders are becoming blurred; "institutions" are giving way to "networks."[12] Just as the Roman empire, with its shifting and uncertain borders, succeeded the Roman republic, the coming age is an "imperial" age, "an age of a diffuse and continuous violence. There will no longer be any territory or frontier to defend, but only order — operating methods — to protect."[13]

A precursor of this may be found in much of the so-called Third World, where decolonization was followed by the yoke of the World Bank and the International Monetary Fund.[14] Furthermore, human society as a whole may be too vast for a political body capable of forming a collective sovereignty that can meet new challenges in as supple a way as nation-states.[15]

Neither Ohmae nor Guéhenno presents a vision that we can rush to defend, because neither offers a plausible solution. Ohmae's apolitical dream world of the four I's surging across obsolete borders fails to take account of human needs beyond the merely economic, and Guéhenno's gloomy conception of the future offers little guidance to those who would seek to build new political structures on the still vital remains of the existing ones. What both do offer, however, are compelling arguments that existing nation-state fealties and responsibilities will not escape the current era unchanged.

The inforoute is one of the agents of the coming changes. By helping break down spatial ideas of community, it weakens some of the bonds that hold nation-states together. Is this a good thing or a bad thing? Is the world heading toward a single, stultifying morass of California-ized cultural expression? Will everything that is valuable and distinctive about individual nation-states be wiped out, after all?

We prefer a more optimistic view. The inforoute may enable Hollywood to complete its spatial conquest of the world and spread the corporate message of consumerism using the magic of satellite communications, penetrating those last jungle hideouts and reaching those final mountain passes and remote plains and hidden urban slums. But at the same time it will give others the chance to spread their own messages to a far broader audience than would have been possible previously.

The 500-channel universe that always seems to be just around the corner will be dominated by U.S. programming but not monopolized by it. Others *will* have a chance to get a word in edgewise, and these others will include Canadian and Third World channels. This is a far cry from current practices in film distribution, as we saw in Chapter 3. The Internet has achieved its greatest penetration in English-speaking and Scandinavian countries, but it is open to all comers, and its offerings span the planet.

It is true that the globalization of information provides new opportunities for Hollywood and everything it stands for, but it also provides many of these same opportunities for Hollywood's competitors, and often at low enough cost for competition to be feasible. Also, regional voices will be heard more often. U.S. content will not necessarily come from Hollywood or New York, and the voice of France will not be just the voice of Paris.

But what happens if our identities cease to be shaped by nation-states or even by region-states? Will the multiplicity of messages, and the increasing ease with which these are captured around the world, lead to an amorphous worldwide information melting pot? We think not. The characteristics and the common interests that shaped different groups of people in different places will not suddenly vanish. Most Canadians still consider themselves Canadians despite nearly a century of bombardment from Hollywood.

What is this national identity that is so fragile and so precious? This matter is complicated by the fact that Canada, like most other so-called nation-states, actually is made up of groups which have much in common but which also have quite separate identities. On the French-speaking side, identity is determined largely by language and its attendant cultural characteristics. On the English-speaking side, Canadians often like to define themselves by distinguishing themselves from Americans in matters such as easier access to medical care and tougher access to firearms. And then there are various indigenous and immigrant groups and regional particularities, each of them adding to Canada's mixture of identities. If the CRTC were to vanish tomorrow and the last remaining trade barriers with the United States were to disappear, would any of this really change?

In economic and environmental terms, there do exist short-term palliative measures that can respond to some of the imbalances that have accompanied globalization. Morris Miller, currently an economic consultant and adjunct professor at the University of Ottawa, neatly summarizes some of these measures in a paper presented at the 1994 Pugwash workshop.[16] These include a global carbon tax on fossil fuels that could be used to finance environmental programs, an issuance by the IMF of special drawing rights to the poorest countries, debt-for-nature swaps that can provide financial relief while enhancing environmental prospects, payment of "rent" by industrialized countries for their disproportionate fouling of the oceans and atmosphere, and a tiny tax on international money transfers (at only 0.003%, such a tax could finance all UN operations, including peacekeeping).[17]

Such measures have been identified with what passes for left-wing academic thinking these days, and indeed Miller shows a healthy skepticism towards the corporate vision of globalization. But as an economist he has an instinctive appreciation of the importance of world trade, and he warns of the need for institutional change, which can come in a controlled and orderly way or, more ominously, in "a retreat from the 40-year-old trend toward interdependence to autocratic policies as each of the industrialized countries endeavours to minimize the damage to itself by adopting 'beggar-thy-neighbour' policies."[18] Finding solutions is urgent.

Globalization of the economy and globalization of information are occurring simultaneously and sometimes, though not always, along parallel tracks. Neither should be viewed as an inescapable threat. Instead, they should be welcomed, as long as certain minimal conditions apply. On the information side, these conditions include an open door for those with material to share or to receive, a separation of content providers and channel providers to maintain diversity and independence and, however unfashionable this may sound in neoliberal circles, oversight by governments and government-controlled international bodies to ensure the broadest possible access to the information highway on both the production and the consumption side. There is a big world out there, and it is ours to share and discover, not to hide from.

Endnotes

Chapter 1

1. Glenn Schneider, "The Wired City," *Last Post*, November 1979, pp. 24–29.
2. George Gilder, "Life after Television, Updated," *Forbes ASAP*, February 23, 1994.
3. Michael Strangelove, *How to Advertise on the Internet: An Introduction to Internet-Facilitated Marketing and Advertising* (Ottawa: Strangelove Internet Enterprises, 1994), pp. 208.
4. Quoted in Peter Otte, *The Information Superhighway: Beyond the Internet* (Indianapolis: Que, 1994), p. 190.
5. George Gilder, "Mike Milken and the Two Trillion Dollar Opportunity," *Forbes ASAP*, May 5, 1995.
6. Schneider, "The Wired City," p. 27.
7. Canada, Information Highway Advisory Council (IHAC), *Final Report: Connection, Community, Content — The Challenge of the Information Highway* (Ottawa: Supply and Services, 1995), p. 11.
8. E.P. Thompson, *The Making of the English Working Class* (1963; New York: Vintage, 1966), pp. 547–602.
9. Robert Heilbroner, ed., *The Essential Adam Smith* (New York: Norton, 1986), p. 298.

Chapter 2

1. "Ursula Major," *This Magazine*, May/June 1996, p. 39.
2. "Spar Takes Key Rogers' Executive as Chief," Toronto *Globe and Mail, Report on Business*, March 12, 1996.
3. "Aircraft Stocks Rise on Merger Talk," reprinted from the *Wall Street Journal*, Toronto *Globe and Mail*, November 17, 1995, p. B9.
4. Richard Gwyn, *The 49th Paradox: Canada in North America* (Toronto: McClelland and Stewart, 1985), p. 51.
5. Walter Laqueur, *A World of Secrets: The Uses and Limits of Intelligence* (New York: Basic Books, 1985), p. 30.
6. Ernie Regehr, *Arms Canada: The Deadly Business of Military Exports* (Toronto: James Lorimer and Co., 1987), pp. 218–30.
7. Robert Reich, *The Work of Nations* (New York: Knopf, 1991), p. 92.
8. James Littleton, *Target Nation* (Toronto: Lester & Orpen Dennys/CBC Enterprises, 1986), p. 24.
9. Alexander Ross, *The Booming Fifties: 1950–1960* (Toronto: Natural Science of Canada, 1977), p. 88.
10. John Sloan Dickey, *Canada and the American Presence: The United States Interest in an Independent Canada* (New York: New York University Press, 1975), p. 77.

11. Robert Chodos and Drummond Burgess, "Ma Bell, and Your Phone Bill and Canada's Newest Multinational Corporation," *Last Post*, March 1974, pp. 22–30.
12. "AT&T's Angry, Tough and Testy," *Toronto Star*, May 10, 1996, p. C-1.
13. Alistair D. Edgar and David G. Haglund, *The Canadian Defence Industry in the New Global Environment* (Montreal and Kingston: McGill-Queen's University Press, 1995).

Chapter 3

1. Richard Schultz, "Comments on Steven Globerman, 'The Economics of the Information Superhighway,' " mimeo (Montreal: McGill University, Department of Political Science, n.d.).
2. Lawrence Surtees, *Wire Wars: The Canadian Fight for Competition in Telecommunications* (Toronto: Prentice Hall Canada, 1994), p. 8.
3. Charles Sirois and Claude E. Forget, *Le médium et les muses: La culture, les télécommunications et l'autoroute de l'information* (Montreal: Institute for Research on Public Policy, 1995), p. 31. In English from the same publisher as *The Medium and the Muse: Culture, Telecommunications and the Information Highway*.
4. Ibid., p. 34.
5. Ibid., p. 57.
6. Ken Auletta, "Selling the Air," *New Yorker*, February 13, 1995, p. 37.
7. Surtees, *Wire Wars*, p. 175.
8. Surtees, *Wire Wars*, pp. 64–5.
9. Quoted in Ibid., p. 170.
10. Ibid., p. 93.
11. Claudia Eller and Sallie Hofmeister, "Hollywood's Wildest Ride: No Year Can Match 1995 for Cataclysmic Activity," *Los Angeles Times*, December 29, 1995, p. D1.
12. From a sidebar to Eller and Hofmeister, "Hollywood's Wildest Ride."
13. Lewis J. Lapham, "Robber Barons Redux," *Harper's*, January 1994, p. 7.
14. Ibid.
15. Leslie Cauley, "Telecom Companies Adopt Defensive Manoeuvres," *Wall Street Journal*, reprinted in the Toronto *Globe and Mail*, March 25, 1996, p. B4.
16. Mark Landler and Geraldine Fabrikant, "Even Before Deregulation, Cable Rates Are on the Rise," *New York Times*, April 12, 1996, p. D1.
17. Geoffrey Rowan, "IBM Canada, Bell Close to Huge Deal," Toronto *Globe and Mail*, February 27, 1996, p. B1.

Chapter 4

1. Steven Levy, "This Changes Everything," *Newsweek*, December 25, 1995/January 1, 1996, p. 26.
2. Ann Landers, "Her Chat-Line Romancer Turned Out to Be a Real-Life Rapist," *Toronto Star*, June 25, 1996.
3. Quoted in Theodore Roszak, *The Cult of Information: A Neo-Luddite Treatise on High-Tech, Artificial Intelligence, and the True Art of Thinking*, 2nd ed. (Berkeley: University of California Press, 1994), p. 186.

4. Howard Rheingold, *The Virtual Community: Homesteading on the Electronic Frontier* (1993; New York: HarperPerennial, 1994), pp. 66–67.
5. Ellen Ullman, "Come In, CQ: The Body on the Wire," in *Wired_women: Gender and New Realities in Cyberspace*, ed. Lynn Cherny and Elizabeth Reba Weise (Seattle: Seal Press, 1996), p. 6.
6. K.K. Campbell, "Get Wired: The Information Highway Is Corporate Crap, but the Internet Is Not," *Eye*, March 10, 1994, pp. 1, 6–7.
7. "What Are We Doing On-line?", *Harper's*, August 1995, p. 41.
8. Michael Strangelove, *How to Advertise on the Internet: An Introduction to Internet-Facilitated Marketing and Advertising* (Ottawa: Strangelove Internet Enterprises, 1994), pp. 19–99.
9. Barbara Love, "Notes on the Economics of New Media," memo to Hershel Sarbin, Cowles Business Media, mimeo, November 2, 1994.
10. Mark Starowicz, "The Gutenberg Revolution of Television: Speculations on the Impact of New Tecnologies," address to the Canadian Embassy, Washington, March 29, 1993, mimeo, p. 6.
11. Canada, Information Highway Advisory Council (IHAC), *Final Report: Connection, Community, Content — The Challenge of the Information Highway* (Ottawa: Supply and Services, 1995), p. 37.
12. Esther Dyson, "Intellectual Value," *Wired*, July 1995, p. 137.
13. Ibid., pp. 141, 182.
14. Canada, IHAC, *Final Report*, p. 48.
15. Robert Jay Lifton, *The Protean Self: Human Resilience in an Age of Fragmentation* (New York: Basic Books, 1993), p. 1.
16. Quoted in Judy Anderson "yduJ", "Not for the Faint of Heart: Contemplations on Usenet," in *Wired_women*, p. 137.
17. Amy S. Bruckman, "Gender Swapping on the Internet," paper presented to INET 1993.
18. Shannon McRae, "Coming Apart at the Seams: Sex, Text and the Virtual Body," in *Wired_women*, p. 257.
19. John Leland, "Bisexuality," *Newsweek*, July 17, 1995, p. 46.
20. Martine Rothblatt, "The Apartheid of Sex: A Manifesto on the Freedom of Gender" (New York: Crown Publishers, 1995), p. 152.
21. Karen Coyle, "How Hard Can It Be?", in *Wired_women*, p. 54.
22. Ellen Lupton, *Mechanical Brides: Women and Machines from Home to Office* (New York: Cooper-Hewitt National Museum of Design/Princeton Architectural Press, 1993), p. 38.
23. "Interview with Mark Poster: Community, New Media, Post-humanism," conducted through e-mail, October 1994, by Erick Heroux and made available through the Internet.
24. Rheingold, *The Virtual Community*, p. 24.
25. John Gray, "Cyberspace Offers a Hollow Freedom," *Guardian Weekly*, April 16, 1995.
26. Robert E. Babe, "The Real World of the Information Highway," *Point of View*, Summer 1994, pp. 17, 19.
27. Ibid., p. 19.
28. See Robert Chodos, Rae Murphy and Eric Hamovitch, *Canada and the Global Economy* (Toronto: James Lorimer and Company, 1993).

29. Suneel Rattan, "A New Divide between Haves and Have-nots?", *Time*, Special Issue, Spring 1995 (Vol. 145, No. 12).
30. Canada, IHAC, *Final Report*, p. 42.
31. Bill Gates, "The Road Ahead," *Newsweek*, November 27, 1995, p. 61.

Chapter 5

1. George Gilder, "Mike Milken and the Two Trillion Dollar Opportunity," *Forbes ASAP*, May 5, 1995.
2. Roger Bird, commentary on Document One, in *Documents of Canadian Broadcasting* (Ottawa: Carleton University Press, 1988), p. 7.
3. Patrick Crawley, "Canadian Production Tradition," unpublished document, July 1, 1996.
4. "CRTC Cult," Toronto *Globe and Mail*, February 15, 1994.
5. Ken Auletta, "John Malone: Flying Alone," *New Yorker*, February 7, 1994, p. 52.
6. Antonia Zerbisias, "The World at Their Feet," August 27, 1995, *Toronto Star*, p. C1.
7. Don Tapscott, "On Ramp," Toronto *Globe and Mail*, January 10, 1994, p. B8.
8. Quoted in Robert E. Babe, *Telecommunications in Canada* (Toronto: University of Toronto Press, 1990), p. 56.
9. Peter C. Newman, *The Canadian Revolution: From Deference to Defiance* (Toronto: Viking, 1995), p. 145.
10. Keith Spicer, "Good TV Can Help Drive Out the Bad," Montreal *Gazette*, October 2, 1995.
11. Harvey Enchin, "Power Drops Plans for Direct TV," Toronto *Globe and Mail*, February 2, 1996, pp. A1–A2.
12. Ibid.
13. Lawrence Surtees, *Wire Wars: The Canadian Fight for Competition in Telecommunications* (Toronto: Prentice Hall Canada, 1994), p. 264.
14. Enchin, "Power Drops Plans."
15. Terence Corcoran, "Just Who Is Setting Satellite Policy?", Toronto *Globe and Mail*, May 11, 1996, p. B2.
16. Jay Bryan, "Thank the CRTC for Lousy, Costly Cable," Montreal *Gazette*, February 6, 1996, p. D7.
17. Charles Sirois and Claude E. Forget, *Le médium et les muses: La culture, les télécommunications et l'autoroute de l'information* (Montreal: Institute for Research on Public Policy, 1995), p. 87. In English from the same publisher as *The Medium and the Muse: Culture, Telecommunications and the Information Highway.*
18. Terence Corcoran, "Telephone Companies Closing in on Rogers," Toronto *Globe and Mail*, March 13, 1994, p. B2.
19. David Crane, *The Next Canadian Century* (Toronto: Stoddart, 1992).

Chapter 6

1. Robert Heilbroner, Exchange of letters with Felix Rohatyn, *New York Review of Books*, October 5, 1995.

2. "The Myth of the Powerless State," *The Economist*, October 7–13, 1995.
3. Peter Drucker, "The Age of Social Transformation," *Atlantic Monthly*, November 1994, p. 53.
4. "Survey: American Business," *The Economist*, September 16–22, 1995, p. 11.
5. Drucker, "Age of Social Transformation," p. 59.
6. Jeremy Rifkin, *The End of Work: The Decline of the Global Labor Force and the Dawn of the Post-Market Era* (New York: G.P. Putnam's Sons, 1995).
7. Quoted in Judy Steed, "The Radical Banker," *Toronto Star*, November 19, 1995, p. D1.
8. Allan Sloan "Excited about the Dow? Get a Grip on Yourself," *Newsweek*, November 27, 1995.
9. Quoted in Rifkin, *The End of Work*.
10. Cited in *The Economist*, December 2–8, 1995, p. 24.
11. "Telecommunications," *The Economist*, September 30–October 6, 1995, p. 63.
12. Peter Cook, "A Working Class in Need of a Voice," Toronto *Globe and Mail, Report on Business*, December 11, 1995.
13. Ibid.
14. Jeremy Brecher, "Global Village or Global Pillage," *The Nation*, December 6, 1993.
15. Robert Reich, "As The World Turns," *New Republic*, May 1, 1989, p. 23.
16. Christopher Lasch, "The Revolt of the Elites: How They Canceled Their Allegiance to America," *Harper's*, November 1994, p. 39.
17. *London Review of Books*, May 13, 1993.
18. Thomas L. Friedman, "When Money Talks, Governments Listen," *New York Times*, July 24, 1994, p. E3.
19. David Coxe, "The Big Picture," Toronto *Globe and Mail, Report on Business*, July 10, 1995.
20. *The Economist*, June 10–16, 1995.
21. Mary Gooderham, "Technology Race Casualties Find They've Nowhere to Go," Toronto *Globe and Mail*, October 11, 1995, p. 1.
22. Canada, Information Highway Advisory Council (IHAC), *Final Report: Connection, Community, Content — The Challenge of the Information Highway* (Ottawa: Supply and Services, 1995), p. 54.
23. Ibid., p. 220.
24. Ibid., pp. 224, 227.
25. Quoted in Judy Steed, "Could We Be Nearing Technology Overload," *Toronto Star*, July 16, 1995.

Chapter 7

1. Ethan B. Kapstein, "Workers and the World Economy," *Foreign Affairs*, May–June 1996, pp. 17, 37.
2. Terence Corcoran, "What's Wrong with Pat Buchanan," Toronto *Globe and Mail*, February 24, 1996, p. B2.
3. *Newsweek*, February 26, 1996, cover; and Allan Sloan, "The Hit Men," Ibid., pp. 44–48.

4. Quoted in Thomas L. Friedman, "The Globalization Game Produces Some Angry Losers," New York Times Service, in St. Petersburg *Times*, February 9, 1996.
5. United States, Department of Commerce, National Telecommunications and Information Administration, *National Information Infrastructure: Agenda for Action* (Washington, 1993).
6. Canada, Information Highway Advisory Council (IHAC), *Final Report: Connection, Community, Content — The Challenge of the Information Highway* (Ottawa: Supply and Services, 1995), p. 18.
7. Kenichi Ohmae, *The End of the Nation State* (New York: Free Press, 1995); Jean-Marie Guéhenno, *The End of the Nation-State*, trans. Victoria Elliott (Minneapolis: University of Minnesota Press, 1995).
8. Ohmae, *End of the Nation State*, p. 2.
9. Ibid., p. 5.
10. Guéhenno, *End of the Nation-State*, pp. x–xiii.
11. Ibid., p. x.
12. Ibid., p. 58–65.
13. Ibid., p. 119.
14. Ibid., p. 2.
15. Ibid., p. xii.
16. Morris Miller, "The Threat and the Promise of Globalization: Can it be Made to Work for a Brighter Future?," Third Pugwash Workshop, Pugwash, N.S., July 28–31, 1994.
17. Ibid., pp. 20–21.
18. Ibid., p. 25.

Suggestions for Further Reading

Ambrose, Stephen E. *The Rise to Globalism: American Foreign Policy since 1938*. London: Penguin, 1988.

Babe, Robert E. *Telecommunciations in Canada*. Toronto: University of Toronto Press, 1990.

Cherny, Lynn, and Weise, Elizabeth Reba, eds. *Wired___women: Gender and New Realities in Cyberspace*. Seattle: Seal Press, 1996.

Crane, David. *The Next Canadian Century*. Toronto: Stoddart, 1992.

Gates, Bill. *The Road Ahead*. New York: Viking, 1995.

Gilder, George. *Life after Television*. Revised edition. New York: W.W. Norton, 1994.

Heilbroner, Robert. *The Worldly Philosophers: The Lives, Times, and Ideas of the Great Economic Thinkers*. Revised edition. New York: Simon and Schuster, 1961.

Johnston, David; Johnston, Deborah; and Handa, Sunny. *Getting Canada Online: Understanding the Information Highway*. Toronto: Stoddart, 1995.

Menzies, Heather. *Whose Brave New World?: The Information Highway and the New Economy*. Toronto: Between the Lines, 1996.

Negroponte, Nicholas. *Being Digital*. New York: Knopf, 1995.

Reich, Robert. *The Work of Nations*. New York: Knopf, 1991.

Rheingold, Howard. *The Virtual Community: Homesteading on the Electronic Frontier*. New York: Addison-Wesley, 1993.

Rifkin, Jeremy. *The End of Work: The Decline of the Global Labor Force and the Dawn of the Post-Market Era.* New York: G.P. Putnam's Sons, 1995.

Sirois, Charles, and Forget, Claude E. *The Medium and the Muse: Culture, Telecommunications and the Information Highway.* Montreal: Institute for Research on Public Policy, 1995.

Surtees, Lawrence. *Wire Wars: The Canadian Fight for Competition in Telecommunications.* Toronto: Prentice Hall Canada, 1994.

Index

A.V. Roe, 24, 86
ABC, 88
Advanced Research Projects Agency (ARPA), 54
Advertising, 58-60, 65
aerospace industry, 17, 21, 24
Air Canada, 94
Aitken, Max (Lord Beaverbrook), 86
Alberta, 114
Alexander, Lamar, 90
Allen, Paul, 45
Allen, Robert E., 128
alliances, multilateral, 40, 46-7
alliances, multilateral. *See also* mergers
AlphaCom, 76
American Airlines, 50
Ameritech, 49
analogue: process, 6; transmission media, 6-7
Anderson, James T., 93
Angus, Ian, 82
Apple, 116
Archie, search tool, 70
ARPANET, 54
AT&T, 8, 23, 25, 32, 38, 41, 45, 46, 47, 49, 49-50, 51, 111,115, 116-7, 128. *See also* Baby Bells
AT&T Canada, 25, 30, 49-50
AT&T Capital, 117
ATMs, 111
audience: bifurcation of, 66; fragmented, 61
Auletta, Ken, 90
auto industry, 112
Avro Arrow, 24, 86

B.C. Telephone, 2
Babe, Robert E., 77-8, 93, 94
Baby Bells, 32, 45, 45-6, 47, 49, 51
balanced budgets, 127
Barlow, John Perry, 1, 56
Barrett, Matthew, 111
BCE, 40, 44, 99, 100
Belanger, Marc, 14
Bell, Alexander Graham, 95
Bell Atlantic, 47
Bell Canada, 2, 8, 11, 23, 25, 30, 38, 42, 43, 51, 52, 81-2,95. *See also* BCE
Bell Sygma, 51

Benimadhu, Prem, 117
Berlusconi, 47
Bernardo-Homolka case, 12
Bertelsmann, 51
Birkerts, Sven, 56
bits, 6
Black, Conrad, 88-9
Blankenhorn, Dana, 8
Boeing, 19, 24
Bombardier, 24
Brander, Roy, 55
Brecher, Jeremy, 118
Bretton Woods Agreement, 120
Britain, 20, 21, 24, 119, 120
British Airways, 115
British Columbia, 114
Bronfman, Edgar, Jr., 46
Bruckman, Amy, 73-4
Bryan, Jim, 101
Buchanan, Pat, 113-4, 127-8, 129
business cycle, 113, 114

Cable: companies (cablecos), 9, 10, 32, 38-9, 42, 51, 60-1, 97, 101; industry, 32-3; local monopolies, 33; modem, 56; rate increase, 49. *See also* Rogers Communications
Canada: aerospace industry, 17, 22, 86; aircraft assembly plants, 21; airline industry, 50; anti-American resentment, 24; and Cold War, 22; components manufacturing, 22, 25; culture, 11-2; defence spending, 22; economic recovery, 114; foreign ownership laws, 50-1; inflation in, 117; magazine publishing in, 62; mixed economy, 95; multimedia empires in, 51-2; national identity, 132-3; newspaper industry, 88-9; and radar technology, 86; radio communication, 85-6; real wages in, 116; role of the state, 18; sovereignty, 11, 12; telecommunications policies, 10-1; telephone industry, 86; and U.S. military economy, 19-26; unemployment, 13; unemployment rate, 113; and vertical integration, 52
Canada customs, 68
Canadair, 24
Canadarm, 17

RADINT, 22
radio: commercial advertising on, 59; elec-
tronic transmission, 6
Rae, Bob, 72
railways: rights-of-way, 5, 30-1; system
of, 20
RAND Corporation, 54
Ratan, Suneel, 80
Raytheon, 19
Reagan, Ronald, 118
recession, 114
Redstone, Sumner, 90
Regehr, Ernie, 22
region states, 130-1
regulation: by government, 8, 9, 85-7, 104-
5; of information highway, 27; state,
91-6; technological change and, 92.
See also state, the
Reich, Robert, 22, 118
Reuther, Walter, 125
Rheingold, Howard, 54, 57, 76-7
Rifkin, Jeremy, 108, 110, 114
rights-of-way, 5, 30-2
Rockefeller, John D., 48
Rogers Cablesystems, 2, 11, 17, 56
Rogers Communications, 38, 40-4, 51,
100, 104
Rogers, Ted, Jr., 40-1, 42
Rogers, Ted, Sr., 41
Rogers Wave system, 56
Roosevelt, Franklin, 20
Ross, Alexander, 93
Rothblatt, Martine, 74
Rothschild, Lord Jacob, 50
Royal Bank of Canada, 111

Saffo, Paul, 1, 70
satellite: broadcasting, 7; direct-to-home,
12, 92, 98-104
Saturday Night, 89
Savoy Pictures, 45
Schmidt, Helmut, 113
Schneider, Glenn, 2, 10
Schultz, Richard, 29
scientific-technological revolution, 92
Seagram Co., 35, 45, 46, 51
Seidel, Michael, 58
service sector, 37-8, 109
Shade, Leslie Regan, 75
Shaw Communications, 42, 104
Siegel, Martha, 58
SIGNIT, 22
Singapore, 129
Sirois, Charles, 33, 35, 104
Sloan, Allan, 112, 128
Slouka, Mark, 56

Smith, Adam, 15, 107, 119
Sony Corp., 46
Sony theaters, 34
Southam, 88, 99
Southwestern Bell (SBC), 45-6, 47
sovereignty, 11-2
Spar Aerospace, 17, 22, 86
Spicer, Keith, 101
Spielberg, Steven, 45
Sports Illustrated, 12
Sprint, 38, 46, 47
Spry, Graham, 85
Stanley, Morgan, 19
Starowicz, Mark, 61
state, the, 15; American, 18, 27; involve-
ment in communications and transpor-
tation, 93-6; and nationalization, 94;
new economy and, 107; protection of
private interests, 87; and public enter-
prise, 18-9; regulation of monopoly,
96-7; as regulator, 91-3; and regulatory
systems, 94-6, 97. *See also* govern-
ments; nation-state; regulation
Steiner, P., 73
Stentor group, 2, 40, 42, 50, 98
Stone, Norman, 12
Strangelove, Michael, 4, 59
Strategic Air Command, 23
Suez crisis, 21
Surtees, Lawrence, 30, 40, 43
Sutherland, David, 55
Swissair, 115

takeovers, 40
Tapscott, Don, 91
taxes, 110, 117
technological innovation, 2-3; backlash
against, 13; concentration of ownership
and, 43; direction of, 14
Tee-Comm Electronics Corp, 99
Tele-Communications Inc. (TCI), 47, 49,
51
Telecom Ireland, 115
telecommunications: Canadian state and,
94; integration of industries, 2, 7, 8,
10; ownership structure of industry,
50-1. *See also* telephone
Teleglobe Inc., 33, 44, 50
telegraph: Canadian system, 86, 93-4; railway companies and, 37
telephone: deregulation of long-distance,
32; electronic transmission, 6; industry
layoffs, 38; local rates, 38; long-distance rates, 38; marketing to women,
76; separation of service and network
ownership, 38; wires, 5, 7

16.1